The Regeneration of the Christian And the Holy Spirit

YOU SHALL RECEIVE POWER

Pastor Cecil Level

xulon PRESS

Copyright © 2011 by Pastor Cecil Level

The Regeneration of the Christian And the Holy Spirit
You Shall Receive Power
by Pastor Cecil Level

Printed in the United States of America

ISBN 9781613798126

All rights reserved solely by the author. The author guarantees all contents are original and do not infringe upon the legal rights of any other person or work. No part of this book may be reproduced in any form without the permission of the author. The views expressed in this book are not necessarily those of the publisher.

Unless otherwise indicated, Bible quotations are taken from The King James Version. Copyright © 1976 by Thomas Nelson, Inc. and The New King James Version. Copyright © 1979, 1980, 1982 by Thomas Nelson, Inc.

To contact Pastor Cecil Level for speaking write:
Pastor Cecil Level
P.O. Box 143206
Fayetteville, Georgia 30214
or email:pastorlevel@gmail.com

www.xulonpress.com

DEDICATION

To My Children,
Cecil, Makeda, and Caleb
And The Employees of City of Atlanta
Fire Rescue Department, Delta Air Lines, and
my entire church family
*who have given me the freedom and
confidence to write this book*

**but most of all
To My Wife Deidra,**

*The angel whose love, understanding,
wisdom, and forgiveness have sustained me
through 30 years of dreams and nightmares*

ACKNOWLEDGEMENT

My deepest thanks go to my entire family starting with my grandparents Ms. Lillie McNally, and Ms. Mable Level, parents Robert and Lillie Level, mother and father in-law, Marshall and Sarah Scruggs. All of my sisters, Ms. Jacqueline Bivings, Bishop Debbie Jordan, Ms. Jan Douglas, Apostle Priscilla Burks brothers, Robert Level, David Level, Kenneth Level, Ahmad Level many nieces, nephews, brother and sister in-laws.

I would like to special acknowledge Dr. Jonathan Greer II who has always been a spiritual father figure in my life and many others. For appreciating my strengths and understanding my weaknesses!

TABLE OF CONTENTS

Preface
The Regeneration of the Christian and the Holy Spirit xi

Forward
Pastor Cecil Level.. xv

Introduction
The Spirit in the Old Testament xxiii

Chapter 1
Who is the Holy Spirit? 29

Chapter 2
What Is the Doctrine of the Trinity? 39

Chapter 3
Why Did the Holy Spirit come?...62

Chapter 4
How is the Holy Spirit Related to every Christian?..............63

Chapter 5
What is the Spirit – Fill Life? 71

Chapter 6
Why Are So Few Christians Fill With the Holy Spirit?..........74

Chapter 7
How Can A Christian Be Filled With the Holy Spirit?...........82

Chapter 8
How Can A Christian Know When He is Filled With
the Holy Spirit? 96

Chapter 9
What Results Can One Expect From Being Filled With
the Holy Spirit? 98

Chapter 10
Is There More Than One Filling of the Holy Spirit? 120

Chapter 11
The Voice of the Spirit 125

The Regeneration of the Christian And the Holy Spirit
YOU SHALL RECEIVE POWER

Has it ever occurred to you that there could be much more to the Christian life than what you are now experiencing?

Jesus said, "I came that they (you and I and all Christians) might have life, and might have it abundantly" (John 10:10). Yet, if you are an average professing Christian, you are undoubtedly thinking, "There is certainly nothing abundant about my life. I try to witness, but no one is interested in what I have to say. I experience nothing but doubts, fears, frustrations and defeat. Surely there must be something more to this Christian life, but I have never found it."

Someone said variety is the spice of life. What makes things exciting is breaking out of the routine, ordinary and familiar and doing something different, especially when it has benefits like the Holy Spirit.

"But ye shall receive power"

In Gen. 12:1-3 and Heb. 11:8-10 Abraham experience the breaking out and doing something different.

Let us look at Abraham who was called the father of faith because he believed, trusted and obeyed God when God told him to leave the familiar which was void of God's presence and step into a new dimension. He left behind the old which was a type of the world and walked into the new which was a type of God's promises.

What made Abraham's decision such a step of faith is the commitment and sacrifice required to make his journey. He was willing to give up what he had for what would be much more, solely on the basis of God's Word.

No one can ever say Abraham's life was dull or boring. Nor can they say Abraham wasn't blessed because of this willingness to step out in faith. He became wealthy, received miracles, negotiated directly with God for his nephew Lot, became the father of an entire nation and had the distinction of being called "the friend of God."

If people are bored as Christians, it's because they have become comfortable where they are and are no longer following the leading of God into exciting new territory of faith. They are no longer trusting God of his promise or obeying his word "But ye shall receive power when the Holy Ghost is come upon you" his word is never void.

Your new territory should be that of the Holy Spirit; The Regeneration of the Christian Receiving power from above. Been able to leave a world that is full of sin and move into a new dimension were his promise stands.

What inside of you is no longer a life of dull or boring but a life full of God's blessings that are willing and ready to receive the Holy Spirit! A part of God's image has been transfer to you.

By breaking out of a life pattern that had no power and moving into a life pattern where power is abundantly. Abraham trusted God to leave the familiar and step into a new dimension. Just as you must leave that of your old presence and walk into the comforter of the Holy Spirit. Moving step by step into your divine life by having unlimited power. God wants you to be where he is omnipresent able to commutate within the spirit without speaking.

This power want be easy, but a true sacrifice.
A journey of receiving miracles and power
well beyond your imagination!
A comforter that will never leave you nor forsake you!
One who will be the Alpha and Omega of your life!

I pray as you read this book that God would lead you into a deeper dimension of his Holy Spirit that the anointing of God would fall upon you and shift you more into his image, his likeness and his ways. Pray now for this divine power.

FORWARD

Because of the evangelistic emphasis on Missions Crusades, I have found it absolutely imperative that each member of our staff, as well as the leaders with whom we work, be filled with the Holy Spirit if we are to have an effective World Wide Mission ministry for Christ.

There was a time in my own Christian ministry when I challenged Christians to witness and live Holy lives for Christ, but the result were so discouraging that I began to devote most of my time and energies to evangelism, where God blessed with much more apparent results. However, as the years have passed, the Holy Spirit has helped me to see the great potential power in lukewarm Christians, if only they are awakened and harnessed for Christ. I am now convinced that the lukewarm, carnal Christian can be changed into a vital, dynamic, witnessing Christian, if he or she will surrender his or her will to Christ and be filled with the Holy Spirit. Again and again

I am reminded of the great contrast between the church of Jesus Christ today and His Church of the first century.

What is the difference? What is the strange quality that sets one man apart from another when both are Christians? Some theologians would say that it is the degree of commitment. Yet there are many people all over the world who are crying out to God, dedicating their lives to Christ day after day, and yet are continuing to be impotent and defeated. Why? Are we not told in Matthew 5:6, "Blessed are those who hunger and thirst for righteousness, for they shall be satisfied"?

Did not John, the beloved disciple, quote Jesus (1 John 1:5-7) as saying that God is light, and in Him is no darkness at all, and that if we walk in the "light" we have fellowship with Father and the Son?

Christians need not live in spiritual poverty. The many thousands of promises recorded in the Word of God apply to every Christian. These promises include: assurance of God's love (John 3:16); eternal life (Romans 6:23); Forgiveness of sin (1 John 1:9); provision of material needs (Philippians 4:19); the ordering of one's steps (Psalms 37:23); the secret of successful prayer (John 15:7); promise of an abundant life (John 10:10); God's promise to honor a holy life (2 Chronicles 16:9); assurance that everything that happens is for our own good (Romans 8:28); deliverance from temptation (1 Corinthians

10:13); victory over fear (1 John 4:18); as well as thousands of others.

The bible promises that every Christian can possess love, joy peace, faith and many other beneficial qualities. What is wrong? Some theologians have stated that at least 90% of all Christians in America are living defeated lives. Others who are in a position to know the spiritual pulse of America have made similar statements. It is quite likely that, according to the law of averages, you are among the 90%. You may have a heart for God. You read your Bible faithfully, you pray, you witness, you are active in your church; yet year after year you continue to fight a losing battle. Temptations come! Half-heartedly you resist, then yield, surrender and are finally defeated. For months you journey in the slough of despondency with Mr. Christian. Then you attend a spiritual retreat and you are back on the Alpine heights for a brief time. Up, down, victories, defeats! Soon you cry out with Paul in Romans 7:24, "Wretched man that I am! Who will set me free from the body of this death?"

As CEO/Founder of Gift For Life World Mission Inc., it is my privilege to spread the Gospel of Jesus Christ and see to the needs of thousands each year. At the conclusion of a message, which I once gave in Accra Ghana West Africa, a devout young man approached me in great concern over his lack of "fruit" in witnessing. "I have tried to witness," he said, "but I have had no results. I read my Bible daily and pray and memorize Scripture. I attend every Christian meeting or Church service; but I have never been able to introduce another to Christ. What is wrong with me?" In counseling with him, I gently probed for the answer to his problem I knew that he meant business. He wanted to please God. He sincerely wanted his friends to know his wonderful Savior, and according to his conduct and Christian activites, he was a model Christian.

Jesus promises in John 14:26 and 16:13 that the Holy Spirit will teach us all things and will guide us into all truth. As I counseled with this young man, we were directed to some very important passages of Scripture. When he claimed these, by faith, they unlocked the door to victory and to unspeakable joy. He left the counseling room rejoicing and with an expectant heart. At that point, he began to experience a fruitful life in Christ such as he had never before known. He knew that something had happened in his life. He was a new man – no longer afraid, impotent and defeated. Now he was bold and had power and faith to believe God. He could hardly wait to see what God was going to do through him. "Lord," he prayed, "who will be the first to whom you will lead me today?"

In the course of the day, the Holy Spirit led this young Christian to a fellow friend to whom he had previously witnessed without apparent success. But today was different.

The Regeneration of the Christian And the Holy Spirit

God had prepared the heart of the other friend and soon these two were bowed in prayer as the friend received Christ. The next day this marvelous experience was repeated with another friend responding as if drawn by an invisible hand. This is not strange, for the Word of God tells us, "No one can come to me, unless the Father draws him" (John 6:44). Through the power of the Holy Spirit, this young man continued to lead fellow friends to Christ day after day. His own life was so wonderfully changed and empowered, so used of God, that he eventually became a Christian minister.

The story of this young man is typical of hundreds of others who have sought across the nation and around the world. There was a young minister who had earned his bachelor's and master's degrees in one of the finest theological seminaries of America, but was ineffective in his witnessing. Upon learning how he could appropriate the power of the Holy Spirit by faith, he experienced a new spirit of expectancy and joy that resulted in a victorious and fruitful life. There was a shy, timid friend of minds at a retreat who expressed this concern for the lost, but was utterly frustrated and defeated by his fear of man. When God's power, victory, love and faith took possession of him, he experienced Joy and fruit such as he had never believed possible. Fear and defeat gave way to courage, radiance and victory. Another faithful witness who heard, believed and received, discovered that witnessing was no longer a duty, but a joy! "It is just like being released from prison," he later exclaimed.

Countless' additional examples such as those cited could be given of others whose fruitless and frustrated lives became fruitful and victorious when they received by faith the power the Holy Spirit and discovered that the promises of Jesus were for them: "Follow Me and I will make you fishers of men" (Matthew 4:19); "By this is My Father glorified, that you bear much fruit" (John 15:8)' "you did not choose Me, but I chose you, and appointed you, that you should go and bear much fruit" (John 15:8); "You did not choose Me, but I chose you, and appointed you, that you should go and bear fruit, and that your fruit should remain: that whatever you ask of the Father in My name, He may give to you" (John 25:16); "And without faith it is impossible to please Him, for he who comes to God must believe that He is, and that He is a rewarded of those who seek Him" (Hebrews 11:6)

Through the centuries there have been followers of Christ who were just ordinary Christians. Nothing spectacular ever happened to them or through them. Then, as happened to Peter and the disciples, something changed their lives. They were no longer ordinary or average. They became men and women of God, instruments of power. Their defeat turned to victory. Doubts and fear turned to assurance, joy and faith becomes fruits of labor.

They were the ones who "turned the world upside down" (Acts 17:6). Cowardly Peter, who denied Jesus three times (you and I have denied Him many more), became the bold Peter of Pentecost who preached fearlessly. On separate occasions, 3,000 and 5,000 believed in Christ and were added to the church. The early disciples possessed a strange new quality of life, a life of power, which transformed the heart of a wicked Roman Empire during the first century.

Their boldness led every one of the twelve to a martyr's grave – expect John, who died in exile on the Isle of Patmos. The change in the lives of those to whom I have just referred all began at Pentecost when those who were gathered together were filled with the Holy Spirit. Through this same power of the Holy Spirit, millions of others through the centuries have been changed into vital, dynamic Christians.

What do you know about the Holy Spirit? What does the Holy Spirit mean to you personally?

Jesus promised in His apostolic commission that the Holy Spirit would give us power to be His witnesses. "But you shall receive power when the Holy Spirit has come upon you; and you shall be my witnesses both in Jerusalem, and in all Jude and Samaria, and even to the remotest part of the earth (Acts 1:8)

IT IS THE PURPOSE OF THIS BOOK TO EXPLAIN HOW TO BE FILLED WITH THE HOLY SPIRIT AS IT RELATES TO THE FULFILLMENT OF THE GREAT COMMISSION OF OUR LORD. THEREFORE, WE SHALL NOT DWELL ON THE MANY OTHER TRUTHS CONCERNING THE ROLE OF THE HOLY SPIRIT IN THE LIFE OF EVERY CHRISTIAN EXCEPT AS THEY CONTRIBUTE TO OUR MAJOR OBJECTIVE.

Let us now consider briefly some of these spiritual truths as they related to the fillings of the Holy Spirit.

Introduction

THE SPIRIT IN THE OLD TESTAMENT

(JOEL 2:28-29) "And it shall come to pass afterward, that I will pour out my spirit upon all flesh; and your sons and your daughters shall prophesy, your old men shall dream dreams, your young men shall see visions: And also upon the servants and upon the handmaids in those days will I pour out my spirit."

The Holy Spirit is one of the three persons of the eternal triune God (see Mark 1:11). Although His full power was not revealed to God's people until the ministry of Jesus and, later, at Pentecost (see Acts 2), there are O.T. passages that refer to Him and His work. This article examines the O.T. teaching about the Holy Spirit. TERM USED. The Hebrew word for "Spirit" is *ruah,* a word that is sometimes translated as "wind" and breath."

Thus, the references in the O.T. to the breath of God or a wind from God (Gen. 2:7; Ezek. 37:9-10,14) can also refer to the work of the Spirit of God.

THE WORK OF THE HOLY SPIRIT IN THE OLD TESTAMENT

The bible describes various activities of the Holy Spirit during O.T. times.

The Holy Spirit had an active role in creation. The second verse of the Bible says that "the spirit of God moved upon the face of the waters" (Gen. 1:2), preparing for the creative word of God to shape the world. Both the Word of God the second person of the Trinity) and the Spirit of God were agents in creation (see Job 26:13; Ps. 33:6). The Spirit is also the author of life. When God created Adam, it was undoubtedly His Spirit that breathed into him the breath of life (Gen. 2:7; Job 27:3), and the Holy Spirit continues to involved in giving life to God's creatures (Job 33:4; Ps. 104:30).

The Spirit was active in communicating God's message to His people. For example, it was the Spirit who instructed the Israelites in the wilderness (Neh. 9:20). When the psalmists of Israel sang their songs, they did so by the Spirit of the Lord (2 Sam. 23:2. Acts 1:16, 20). Similarly, the prophets were inspired by the Spirit of God to declare God's word to the people (Num. 11:29; 1 Sam. 10:5-6; 2 Chr. 20:14; 24:`9-20; Neh. 9:30; Is. 61:1-3; Mic. 3:8; Zech. 7:12, 2 pet. 1:20-21). According to Ezekiel, one clue to detecting false prophets is that they "follow their own spirit" rather than the Spirit of God (Ezek. 13:2-3); note, though, that it was possible for God's Spirit to come upon someone who was not in a right relationship with Him in order to speak a true message regarding God's people (see Num. 24:2,).

The leadership of God's people in the O.T. was energized by the Spirit of the Lord. Moses, for example, was one with the Spirit of God to such an extent that he shared the very feelings of God, suffering when He suffered and grieving when He grieved at sin (see Ex. 33:11; Ex. 32:19). When Moses obediently chose seventy elders to help nun lead the Israelites, God took the Spirit that was on Moses and put it on them (Num. 11:16-17; see 11:12,). Similarly, when Joshua was commissioned to succeed Moses as leader, God indicated that "the spirit" (the Holy Spirit) was in him (Num. 27:18,). The same Spirit came upon Gideon (Judg. 6:34), David (1 Sam. 16:13), and Zerubbabel (Zech. 4:6). In other words, in the O.T. the greatest qualification needed for leadership was the presence of the Spirit of God.

The Spirit of God could also come upon individuals to equip them for special service. A notable example in the O.T. was Joseph, who was given the Spirit to enable him to function effectively in Pharaoh's cabinet (Gen. 41:38). Also note Bazaleel and Aholiab, whom God filled with His Spirit in order to do the artistic work needed for the construction of the tabernacle and to teach others also (see Ex. 31:1-11; 35:30-35). The idea of "being filled with the Holy Spirit" here is not precisely the same as the baptism in the Holy Spirit in the N.T. In the O.T., in other words, the Holy Spirit came upon and empowered only a few select individuals chosen for special service to God (see Ex. 31:3, note). The Spirit of the Lord came upon many of the judges, such as Othniel (Judg. 3:9-10), Gideon (Judg. 6:34), Jephthah (Judg. 11:29), and Samson (Judg. 14:5-6; 15:14-16). These examples reveal God's enduring principle that when He chooses to use people greatly, the Spirit of the Lord comes upon them.

There was also awareness in the O.T. that the Spirit desired to lead a person along the paths of righteous living. David testified to this in some of his psalms (Ps. 51:10-13; 143:10). God's people who followed their own way instead of listening to God were really refusing to follow the way of the Spirit (see Gen. 16:2,). Those who failed to live by the Spirit of God inevitably experienced some form of God's judgment (see Num. 14:29, note; Deut. 1:26,)

It should be noted that in O.T. times the Holy Spirit came upon or filled only a few people, empowering them for service or prophecy. There was no general outpouring of the

Holy Spirit on all Israel (Joel 2:28-29; Acts 2:4,16-18). The outpouring of the Spirit in this larger sense did not begin until the great day of Pentecost (Acts 2).

THE PROMISE OF THE FULL POWER OF THE SPIRIT

The O.T. looks forward to the coming age of the Spirit, the N.T. age

On several occasions, the prophets prophesied about the role that the Spirit would play in the life of the coming Messiah. Isaiah especially characterized the coming King and Servant of the Lord as one on whom the Spirit of God would rest in a special way (see Is. 11:1-2; 42:1; 61:1-3). When Jesus read the words from Is. 61 in His hometown synagogue at Nazareth, He ended with: "this day is the scripture fulfilled in your ears" (Luke 4:21).

Other O.T. prophecies looked forward to the time when there would be a general outpouring of the Holy Spirit on all God's people. Most prominent among these passages is Joel 2:28-29, a text quoted on the day of Pentecost by Peter (Acts 2:17-18). But the same message can also be found in Is. 32:15-17; 44:3-5; 59:20-21; Ezek. 11:19-20; 36:26-27; 37:14; 39:29. God promised that when the life and power of His Spirit would come upon His people, they would be enabled to prophesy see visions, have prophetic dreams, live a life of obedience, holiness, and righteousness, and witness with great power. Thus, the O.T. prophets foresaw and prophesied about the age of the Messiah when the outpouring and filling of the Holy Spirit among all humanity would take place. It finally did happen on Pentecost Sunday (ten days after Jesus ascended into heaven), with a subsequent great harvest of salvation (Joel 2:28,32; Acts 2:41; 4:4; 13:44,48-49).

WHO IS THE HOLY SPIRIT?

Since Pentecostals are identified by a strong emphasis on the Holy Spirit, the question arises, what or who is the Holy Spirit? The Holy Spirit is the third person of the Trinity; Father, Son and Holy Spirit. Various groups have defined the Holy Spirit as an abstract principle, an impersonal force, a fluid-like substance, an angel, a subordinate divine being, or the third person in a triune Godhead.

He is not some vague, ethereal shadow or an impersonal force. He is equal in every way with the Father and with the Son. All of the divine attributes are ascribed to the Holy Spirit. He has infinite intellect (1 Corinthians 2:11), will (1 Corinthians 12:11) and emotion (Romans 15:30). But what does the Bible say?

I Pastor Cecil Level describe the Holy Spirit as the "the Commander in-Chief of the Army of Christ. He is the Lord of the harvest, supreme in revival, evangelism and missionary endeavor. Without His consent, plans are bound to fail. It behooves us as Christians to fit our tactical operations into the plan of His strategy, which is the reviving of the church and the evangelization of the world."

The first reference to the Holy Spirit is made in Gen. 1:2. His influence is noted throughout the Old Testament, but it becomes more pronounced in the life and ministry of our Lord Finally, after our Savior ascended to be at the right hand of the Father, the place of power, He sent the Holy Spirit to be the "comforter" or "helper" (John 14:26 and 15:26). The Greek word for comforter or helper is Paraclete, meaning the "one called along beside" the Christian as a companion and friend, also the one who "energizes," "strengthens" and "empowers" the believer in Christ.

GOD IN SPIRITUAL ACTIVITY

God is "the Holy One" (Isaiah 54:5). Only God is holy in Himself; all other Holy beings derive their holiness from Him. Furthermore, God is Spirit (John 4:24), and there is only one Spirit of God (Ephesians 4:4). The title of Holy Spirit describes the fundamental character of God's nature, for holiness forms the basis of His moral attributes while spirituality forms the basis of His non-moral attributes. Thus it describes God Himself, the one Holy Spirit.

For example, Peter told Ananias and Sapphira that they had lied to "to the Holy Ghost" and then said they had lied "unto God" (Acts 5:3-4). Similarly Paul wrote, "Know ye not that ye are the temple of God, and that the Spirit of God dwelleth in you?" and then, "What? know ye not that your body is the temple of the Holy Ghost?" (1 Corinthians 3:16; 6:19).

The Bible calls the Holy Spirit "the Spirit of the LORD (Jehovah), "my (Jehovah) spirit," "the Spirit of God" and "his (God's) Holy Spirit" (Isaiah 40:13; Joel 2:28; Romans 8:9; I Thessalonians 4:8). These phrases show that the Spirit is not distinct from God but rather pertains to God or is God Himself in Spiritual essence. For example, when we speak of the spirit of a man, we do not refer to another person but to the inward nature of the man himself. The man is his spirit and vice versa.

The Bible compares a man and his spirit to God and His Spirit: "For what man knoweth the things of a man, save the spirit of man which is in him? even so the things of God knoweth no man, but the Spirit of God" (I Corinthians 2:11). The former is not two persons, and neither is the latter. We speak of a man's spirit in order to refer to his thoughts, character, or nature, but we do not thereby mean that his spirit is a different person from him or is any less than the total personality. Nor does speaking of God and His Spirit introduce a personal distinction or plurality in Him.

If the Holy Spirit is God Himself, why is this additional designation needed? What distinction of meaning is intended? The title specifically refers to God in spiritual activity, particularly as He works in ways that only a Spirit can.

The first biblical mention of the Spirit is a good example. Genesis 1:1, speaking in general terms, says, "God created the heaven and the earth." Genesis 1:2, focusing on a specific act of God, says, "And the Spirit of God moved upon the face of the waters." Important spiritual activities of God are regenerating, indwelling, sanctifying, and anointing humanity; thus we usually speak of the Holy Spirit in connection with them. (See Acts 1:5-8.)

The roles of Father, Son, and Holy Spirit are necessary to God's plan of redemption for fallen humanity. In order to save us, God had to provide a sinless Man who could die in our place—the Son. In begetting the Son and in relating to humanity, God is the Father. And in working in our lives to transform and empower us, God is the Holy Spirit.

We should note that the titles "Holy Ghost" and "Holy Spirit" are interchangeable; both are translations of the same Greek phrase. The King James Version uses the former more frequently, but it also uses the latter. (See Luke 11:13; Ephesians 1:13; 4:30.) The latter is usually more understandable to modern English speakers, especially those unfamiliar with the Bible. Frequently, the Bible simply speaks of "the Spirit."

THE SPIRIT OF THE FATHER

The Bible identifies the Father and the Holy Spirit as one and the same being. The title of Holy Spirit simply describes what the Father is. There is only one God (Deuteronomy 6:4). The "only true God" is the Father (John 17:3), and He is Spirit (John 4:24).

The Holy Spirit is the Spirit of the Father, not a different person from the Father. For example, Jesus said that in times of persecution God would give us proper words to say, "for it is not ye that speak, but the Spirit of your Father which speaketh in you" (Matthew 10:20).

Jesus spoke of God as our Father in terms of personal relationship, but with reference to supernatural indwelling and anointing Jesus spoke of God as the Holy Spirit.

By definition, the one who begets (causes conception) is the father of the one begotten. The Holy Spirit is literally the Father of Jesus, for Jesus was conceived by the Holy Spirit (Matthew 1:18, 20). If the Father and the Holy Spirit were two persons, then Jesus would have two fathers. When the Bible speaks of the man Christ Jesus in relationship to God it uses the title of Father, but when it speaks of God's action in causing the baby Jesus to be conceived it uses the title of Holy Ghost so that there will be no mistake about the supernatural, spiritual nature of this work.

THE SPIRIT OF JESUS CHRIST

In Jesus Christ dwells all the fullness of the Godhead bodily (Colossians 2:9). Thus the Holy Spirit is literally the Spirit that was in the man Jesus Christ.

All of Christendom confesses that Jesus is Lord, and II Corinthians 3:17 plainly identify the Lord as the Spirit: "Now the Lord is that Spirit: and where the Spirit of the Lord is, there is liberty." The Bible also describes the Holy Spirit as "the Spirit of Christ," "the Spirit of his (God's) Son," and "the Spirit of Jesus Christ" (Romans 8:9; Galatians 4:6; Philippians 1:19). The way that Christ dwells in our hearts is as the Holy Spirit (Romans 8:9-11; Ephesians 3:14-17).

"Another Comforter"

Trinitarians often point to John 14:16 as evidence that the Holy Spirit is a distinct person: "I will pray the Father, and he shall give you another Comforter, that he may abide with you forever." But the context reveals that Jesus was speaking of Himself in another form—in Spirit rather than in flesh.

In the next verse He identified the Comforter as someone who already dwelt with the disciples: "Even the Spirit of truth; whom the world cannot receive, because it seeth him not, neither knoweth him: but ye know him; for he dwelleth with you, and shall be in you" (John 14:17).

Jesus was the One whom they knew and who dwelt with them. The difference was that the Comforter would soon come in them, in a new relationship of spiritual indwelling rather than physical accompaniment.

And in the following verse Jesus plainly identified Himself as the Comforter: "I will not leave you comfortless: I will come to you" (John 14:18).

Some trinitarians try to avoid this clear designation by saying Jesus was speaking of His physical return, either by the Resurrection or the Second Coming, but both explanations ignore the immediate context. Moreover, the Resurrection would have fulfilled the promise only for forty days, while the Second Coming would not have fulfilled the promise for many centuries, long after the listeners' deaths. Clearly, Jesus spoke of coming and abiding in Spirit, as parallel promises show: "Where two or three are gathered together in my name, there am I in the midst of them" (Matthew 18:20); "I am with you alway, even unto the end of the world" (Matthew 28:20).

"HE SHALL NOT SPEAK OF HIMSELF"

Trinitarians also point to John 16:13 as evidence for an independent personality of the Holy Spirit: "Howbeit when he, the Spirit of truth, is come, he will guide you into all truth: for he shall not speak of himself; but whatsoever he shall hear, that shall he speak: and he will shew you things to come." The Greek text literally says, "He will not speak from Himself," meaning, "He will not speak on His own authority" (NKJV).

A trinitarian explanation of the verse is inadequate, however, for the third person would be in a very subordinate role and possibly would not even be omniscient, contrary to the trinitarian doctrine of coequality. He would not be able to say or know anything except what he received from another person. How then could this third person be God and have the power of God? In fact, this verse says the Spirit does not have independent authority or identity. He does not come under another name but in Jesus' name (John 14:26).

In actuality, Jesus was describing the baptism of the Holy Spirit and the working of the Spirit in the believer. (See John 16:7.) It seems that He was trying to counter the tendency that sometimes arises among Spirit-filled people to think that they have some kind of supernatural authority in their own right. In other words, people who receive the Holy Spirit do not thereby have authority to establish any doctrine or teaching of their own. Though they may exercise the gifts of prophecy, tongues, and interpretation of tongues, the Spirit within them will not speak as a separate entity residing within them. Rather, the Spirit in them will only speak what is communicated by the mind of God-what is consistent with the Word of God.

To that extent, John 16:13 makes a conceptual (but not personal) distinction between God as Father, Lord, and Omniscient Mind and God in action, operation, or indwelling. The distinction is similar to that in Romans 8:26-27 and I Corinthians 2:10-16. The latter passage says we can know the mind of God by having the Spirit of God in us, for the Spirit of God knows the things of God. But, as we have already seen, the passage clearly does not envisage a personal distinction in the Godhead, for it compares God and His Spirit to a man and his spirit.

Romans 8:26-27 says, "The Spirit itself maketh intercession for us with groanings which cannot be uttered. And he that searcheth the hearts knoweth what is the mind of the Spirit, because he maketh intercession for the saints according to the will of God." In other words, when the Spirit prompts us and speaks through us in intercessory prayer, we can have confidence that our prayers are in God's will. The Spirit of God will certainly make intercession in accordance with the will of God, for the Spirit is God Himself working in our lives. God will act in harmony with Himself as He first motivates our prayers and then hears and answers our prayers.

Conclusion

Christians are sometimes accused of glorifying the Holy Spirit at the expense of Jesus Christ. Oneness Christians are certainly not guilty of this charge, for we recognize that God is one Spirit and that the Holy Spirit is the Spirit of the risen, living Christ. Receiving the Holy Spirit is the way we receive Jesus Christ into our lives.

We do not have two or three divine spirits in our hearts, nor can we identify distinct religious experiences with each of three divine persons. Both the Bible and personal experience tell us that there is one Spirit, the Spirit of our Lord and Savior Jesus Christ. As our Father, God has told us how to live; in the Son God has shown us how to live and provided an atonement for our sins; and as the indwelling Holy Spirit God enables us to live for Him every day.

What Is The Doctrine of the Trinity?

The doctrine of the Trinity is foundational to the Christian faith. It is crucial for properly understanding what God is like, how He relates to us, and how we should relate to Him. But it also raises many difficult questions. How can God be both one and three? Is the Trinity a contradiction? If Jesus is God, why do the Gospels record instances where He prayed to God?

While we cannot fully understand everything about the Trinity (or anything else), it is possible to answer questions like these and come to a solid grasp of what it means for God to be three in one.

What does it mean that God is a Trinity?

The doctrine of the Trinity means that there is one God who eternally exists as three distinct Persons--the Father, Son, and Holy Spirit. Stated differently, God is one in essence and three in person. These definitions express three crucial truths: (1) The Father, Son, and Holy Spirit are distinct Persons, (2) each Person is fully God, (3) there is only one God.

The Father, Son, and Holy Spirit are distinct Persons. The Bible speaks of the Father as God (Phil. 1:2), Jesus as God (Titus 2:13), and the Holy Spirit as God (Acts 5:3-4). Are these just three different ways of looking at God, or simply ways of referring to three different roles that God plays?

The answer must be no, because the Bible also indicates that the Father, Son, and Holy Spirit are distinct Persons. For example, since the Father sent the Son into the world (John 3:16), He cannot be the same person as the Son. Likewise, after the Son returned to the Father (John 16:10), the Father and the Son sent the Holy Spirit into the world (John 14:26; Acts 2:33). Therefore, the Holy Spirit must be distinct from the Father and the Son.

In the baptism of Jesus, we see the Father speaking from heaven and the Spirit descending from heaven in the form of a dove as Jesus comes out of the water (Mark 1:10-11). In John 1:1 it is affirmed that Jesus is God and, at the same time, that

He was "with God"-thereby indicating that Jesus is a distinct Person from God the Father (cf. also 1:18). And in John 16:13-15 we see that although there is a close unity between them all, the Holy Spirit is also distinct from the Father and the Son.

The fact that the Father, Son, and Holy Spirit are distinct Persons means, in other words, that the Father is not the Son, the Son is not the Holy Spirit, and the Holy Spirit is not the Father. Jesus is God, but He is not the Father or the Holy Spirit. The Holy Spirit is God, but He is not the Son or the Father. They are different Persons, not three different ways of looking at God.

The personhood of each member of the Trinity means that each Person has a distinct center of consciousness. Thus, they relate to each other personally--the Father regards Himself as "I," while He regards the Son and Holy Spirit as "You." Likewise the Son regards Himself as "I," but the Father and the Holy Spirit as "You."

Often it is objected that "If Jesus is God, then he must have prayed to himself while he was on earth." But the answer to this objection lies in simply applying what we have already seen. While Jesus and the Father are both God, they are different Persons. Thus, Jesus prayed to God the Father without praying to Himself. In fact, it is precisely the continuing dialog between the Father and the Son (Matthew 3:17; 17:5; John 5:19; 11:41-42; 17:1ff) which furnishes the best evidence that they are distinct Persons with distinct centers of consciousness.

Sometimes the Personhood of the Father and Son is appreciated, but the Personhood of the Holy Spirit is neglected. Sometimes the Spirit is treated more like a "force" than a Person. But the Holy Spirit is not an it, but a He (see John 14:26; 16:7-15; Acts 8:16). The fact that the Holy Spirit is a Person, not an impersonal force (like gravity), is also shown by the fact that He speaks (Hebrews 3:7), reasons (Acts 15:28), thinks and understands (1 Corinthians 2:10-11), wills (1 Corinthians 12:11), feels (Ephesians 4:30), and gives personal fellowship (2 Corinthians 13:14). These are all qualities of personhood. In addition to these texts, the others we mentioned above make clear that the Personhood of the Holy Spirit is distinct from the Personhood of the Son and the Father. They are three real persons, not three roles God plays.

Another serious error people have made is to think that the Father became the Son, who then became the Holy Spirit. Contrary to this, the passages we have seen imply that God always was and always will be three Persons. There was never a time when one of the Persons of the Godhead did not exist. They are all eternal.

While the three members of the Trinity are distinct, this does not mean that any is inferior to the other. Instead, they are all identical in attributes. They are equal in power, love, mercy, justice, holiness, knowledge, and all other qualities.

Each Person is fully God. If God is three Persons, does this mean that each Person is "one-third" of God? Does the Trinity mean that God is divided into three parts?

The Trinity does not divide God into three parts. The Bible is clear that all three Persons are each one hundred percent God. The Father, Son, and Holy Spirit are all fully God. For example, it says of Christ that "in Him all the fullness of Deity dwells in bodily form" (Colossians 2:9). We should not think of God as like a "pie" cut into three pieces, each piece representing a Person. This would make each Person less than fully God and thus not God at all. Rather, "the being of each Person is equal to the whole being of God."[1] The divine essence is not something that is divided between the three persons, but is fully in all three persons without being divided into "parts."

Thus, the Son is not one-third of the being of God; He is all of the being of God. The Father is not one-third of the being of God; He is all of the being of God. And likewise with the Holy Spirit. Thus, as Wayne Grudem writes, "When we speak of the Father, Son, and Holy Spirit together we are not speaking of any greater being than when we speak of the Father alone, the Son alone, or the Holy Spirit alone."[2]

There is only one God. If each Person of the Trinity is distinct and yet fully God, then should we conclude that there is more than one God? Obviously we cannot, for Scripture is clear that there is only one God: "There is no other God besides me, a righteous God and a Savior; there is none besides me. Turn to me and be saved, all the ends of the earth! For I am God, and there is no other" (Isaiah 45:21-22; see also 44:6-8; Exodus 15:11; Deuteronomy 4:35; 6:4-5; 32:39; 1 Samuel 2:2; 1 Kings 8:60).

Having seen that the Father, the Son, and the Holy Spirit are distinct Persons, that they are each fully God, and that there is nonetheless only one God, we must conclude that all three Persons are the same God. In other words, there is one God who exists as three distinct Persons.

If there is one passage which most clearly brings all of this together, it is Matthew 28:19: "Go therefore and make disciples of all the nations, baptizing them in the name of the Father and the Son and the Holy Spirit." First, notice that the Father, Son, and Holy Spirit are distinguished as distinct Persons. We baptize into the name of the Father and the Son and the Holy Spirit. Second, notice that each Person must be deity because they are all placed on the same level. In fact, would Jesus have us baptize in the name of a mere creature? Surely not. Therefore each of the Persons into whose name we are to be baptized must be deity. Third, notice that although the three divine Persons are distinct, we are baptized into their name (singular), not names (plural). The three Persons are distinct, yet only constitute one name. This can only be if they share one essence.

Is the Trinity Contradictory?

This leads us to investigate more closely a very helpful definition of the Trinity which I mentioned earlier: God is one in essence, but three in Person. This formulation can show us why there are not three Gods, and why the Trinity is not a contradiction.

In order for something to be contradictory, it must violate the law of noncontradiction. This law states that A cannot be both A (what it is) and non-A (what it is not) at the same time and in the same relationship. In other words, you have contradicted yourself if you affirm and deny the same statement. For example, if I say that the moon is made entirely of cheese but then also say that the moon is not made entirely of cheese, I have contradicted myself.

Other statements may at first seem contradictory but are really not. Theologian R.C. Sproul cites as an example Dickens' famous line, "It was the best of times, it was the worst of times." Obviously this is a contradiction if Dickens means that it was the best of times in the same way that it was the worst of times. But he avoids contradiction with this statement because he means that in one sense it was the best of times, but in another sense it was the worst of times.

Carrying this concept over to the Trinity, it is not a contradiction for God to be both three and one because He is not three and one in the same way. He is three in a different way than He is one. Thus, we are not speaking with a forked tongue-we are not saying that God is one and then denying that He is one by saying that He is three. This is very important: God is one and three at the same time, but not in the same way.

How is God one? He is one in essence. How is God three? He is three in Person. Essence and person are not the same thing. God is one in a certain way (essence) and three in a different way (person). Since God is one in a different way than He is three, the Trinity is not a contradiction. There would only be a contradiction if we said that God is three in the same way that He is one.

So a closer look at the fact that God is one in essence but three in person has helped to show why the Trinity is not a contradiction. But how does it show us why there is only one God instead of three? It is very simple: All three Persons are one God because, as we saw above, they are all the same essence. Essence means the same thing as "being." Thus, since God is only one essence, He is only one being-not three. This should make it clear why it is so important to understand that all three Persons are the same essence. For if we deny this, we have denied God's unity and affirmed that there is more than one being of God (i.e., that there is more than one God).

What we have seen so far provides a good basic understanding of the Trinity. But it is possible to go deeper. If we can understand more precisely what is meant by essence and person, how these two terms differ, and how they relate, we will then have a more complete understanding of the Trinity.

Essence and Person

Essence. What does essence mean? As I said earlier, it means the same thing as being. God's essence is His being. To be even more precise, essence is what you are. At the risk of sounding too physical, essence can be understood as the "stuff" that you "consist of." Of course we are speaking by analogy here, for we cannot understand this in a physical way about God. "God is spirit" (John 4:24). Further, we clearly should not think of God as "consisting of" anything other than divinity. The "substance" of God is God, not a bunch of "ingredients" that taken together yield deity.

Person. In regards to the Trinity, we use the term "Person" differently than we generally use it in everyday life. Therefore it is often difficult to have a concrete definition of Person as we use it in regards to the Trinity. What we do not mean by Person is an "independent individual" in the sense that both

I and another human are separate, independent individuals who can exist apart from one another.

What we do mean by Person is something that regards himself as "I" and others as "You." So the Father, for example, is a different Person from the Son because He regards the Son as a "You," even though He regards Himself as "I." Thus, in regards to the Trinity, we can say that "Person" means a distinct subject which regards Himself as an "I" and the other two as a "You." These distinct subjects are not a division within the being of God, but "a form of personal existence other than a difference in being."[3]

How do they relate? The relationship between essence and Person, then, is as follows. Within God's one, undivided being is an "unfolding" into three personal distinctions. These personal distinctions are modes of existence within the divine being, but are not divisions of the divine being. They are personal forms of existence other than a difference in being. The late theologian Herman Bavinck has stated something very helpful at this point: "The persons are modes of existence within the being; accordingly, the Persons differ among themselves as the one mode of existence differs from the other, and-using a common illustration-as the open palm differs from a closed fist."[4]

Because each of these "forms of existence" are relational (and thus are Persons), they are each a distinct center of consciousness, with each center of consciousness regarding Himself as "I" and the others as "You." Nonetheless, these three Persons all "consist of" the same "stuff" (that is, the same "what," or essence). As theologian and apologist Norman Geisler has explained it, while essence is what you are, person is who you are. So God is one "what" but three "whos."

The divine essence is thus not something that exists "above" or "separate from" the three Persons, but the divine essence is the being of the three Persons. Neither should we think of the Persons as being defined by attributes added on to the being of God. Wayne Grudem explains:

But if each person is fully God and has all of God's being, then we also should not think that the personal distinctions are any kind of additional attributes added on to the being of God . . . Rather, each person of the Trinity has all of the attributes of God, and no one Person has any attributes that are not possessed by the others. On the other hand, we must say that the Persons are real, that they are not just different ways of looking at the one being of God...the only way it seems possible to do this is to say that the distinction between the persons is not a difference of `being' but a difference of `relationships.' This is something far removed from our human experience, where every different human `person' is a different being as well. Somehow God's being is so much greater than ours that within his one undivided being there can be an unfolding into interpersonal relationships, so that there can be three distinct persons.[5]

Trinitarian Illustrations?

There are many illustrations which have been offered to help us understand the Trinity. While there are some illustrations which are helpful, we should recognize that no illustration is perfect. Unfortunately, there are many illustrations which are not simply imperfect, but in error. One illustration to beware of is the one which says "I am one person, but I am a student, son, and brother. This explains how God can be both one and three." The problem with this is that it reflects a heresy called modalism. God is not one person who plays three different roles, as this illustration suggests. He is one Being in three Persons (centers of consciousness), not merely three roles. This analogy ignores the personal distinctions within God and mitigates them to mere roles.

Summary

Let us quickly review what we have seen.
    1. The Trinity is not belief in three gods. There is only one God, and we must never stray from this.

2. This one God exists as three Persons.
3. The three Persons are not each part of God, but are each fully God and equally God. Within God's one undivided being there is an unfolding into three interpersonal relationships such that there are three Persons. The distinctions within the Godhead are not distinctions of His essence and neither are they something added on to His essence, but they are the unfolding of God's one, undivided being into three interpersonal relationships such that there are three real Persons.
4. God is not one person who took three consecutive roles. That is the heresy of modalism. The Father did not become the Son and then the Holy Spirit. Instead, there have always been and always will be three distinct persons in the Godhead.
5. The Trinity is not a contradiction because God is not three in the same way that He is one. God is one in essence, three in Person.

Application

The Trinity is first of all important because God is important. To understand more fully what God is like is a way of honoring God. Further, we should allow the fact that God is triune to deepen our worship. We exist to worship God. And God seeks people to worship Him in "spirit and truth" (John 4:24). Therefore we must always endeavor to deepen our worship of God-in truth as well as in our hearts.

The Trinity has a very significant application to prayer. The general pattern of prayer in the Bible is to pray to the Father through the Son and in the Holy Spirit (Ephesians 2:18). Our fellowship with God should be enhanced by consciously knowing that we are relating to a tri-personal God!

Awareness of the distinct role that each Person of the Trinity has in our salvation can especially serve to give us greater comfort and appreciation for God in our prayers, as well as helping us to be specific in directing our prayers. Nonetheless, while recognizing the distinct roles that each Person has, we should never think of their roles as so separate that the other Persons are not involved. Rather, everything that one Person is involved in, the other two are also involved in, one way or another.

Notes

1. Wayne Grudem, Systematic Theology: An Introduction to Biblical Doctrine, (InterVarsity Press and Zondervan Publishing House, 1994), p. 255, emphasis added.
2. Ibid, 252.
3. Ibid, p. 255. While I believe that this is a helpful definition,

it should be recognized that Grudem himself is offering this as more of an explanation than definition of Person.
4. Herman Bavinck, The Doctrine of God, (Great Britain: The Banner of Truth Trust, 1991 edition), p. 303.
5. Grudem, pp. 253-254.

Further Resources

Augustine, On the Trinity
Herman Bavinck, The Doctrine of God, pp. 255-334
Edward Bickersteth, The Trinity.
Wayne Grudem, Systematic Theology, chapter 14
Donald Macleod, Shared Life: The Trinity and the Fellowship of God's People
R.C. Sproul, The Mystery of the Holy Spirit
R.C. Sproul, Essential Truths of the Christian Faith, pp. 35-36
J.I. Packer, Knowing God, pp. 57-63.
John Piper, The Pleasures of God, chapter 1
James White, The Forgotten Trinity

Now let us look at The Doctrine of the Trinity in another aspect view when it comes to God been three persons. This aspect comes from an open argument about God been three persons.

The Trinity

You deserve to know!!! Although many people do not know where the doctrine of "The Trinity" comes from, they accept it as part of the Bible. Many people accept this doctrine because it is the teaching of their church. Many accept it because they have been taught about the trinity for many years, so it must be right. Others accept this teaching only because they don't know of any other teaching concerning God.

We believe that if people actually knew where this teaching originated from, they would not accept it. The trinity was not taught by the Apostles of the Bible. Jesus didn't teach about a trinity. The number three is never used in association with God. Still, most Christians believe in a trinity. Could so many people all be wrong?

YES!!!

Here are the FACTS.

Several hundred years before Jesus was ever born, lived a man named Socrates. He was a philosopher, a man who sought for wisdom. He received his wisdom from an "internal sign"(1), which he considered to be "divine"(2). It spoke to him in "a kind of voice"(3). We would like to believe that it was God speaking to him, but it wasn't.

The Regeneration of the Christian And the Holy Spirit

When asked if these "voices" were Zeus, Apollo, and Athena (3 Greek gods), Socrates said, "Certainly". When asked if they were his gods, he answered, "My lords and ancestors"(4). This man was not in communication with the God of the Bible.

He explained that his wisdom came from these spirits that were "knowing or wise". He openly declared that these wise spirits were demons(5). He esteemed these wise ones, these greek gods, these demons, and they were the source of his wisdom.

Socrates had a famous student named Plato. He was born in 427 B.C. in Athens, Greece. He taught and believed many things that are against the Bible. One example was his idea that there is a universal deity composed of three separate beings. He never called his deity a trinity, but his concept of God was referred to as the "Platonic Trinity". The three persons in this triad were: God, the Ideas, and the World Spirit. These were almost identical to Socrates' gods: Zeus, "the Father"(6); Apollo, the begotten son of Zeus who was the "god of intellect";(7) and Athena whose name means, "eternal life", who was an un-begotten spirit-being who came into the world from the head of Zeus (8).Thus in the teachings of Plato, we have a pagan trinity of gods: father, begotten son, and un-begotten spirit.

Plato also had a famous student, Aristotle. Aristotle taught Alexander the Great, and as a result, this philosophy spread

The Regeneration of the Christian And the Holy Spirit

throughout the world. These philosophies were existed in the days of Jesus Christ, and in the centuries that followed. Although the Apostles who preached the truths found in the Bible were not influenced by these men and their teachings, other men were.

As the church left the time of the apostles, men began introducing teachings that were different from the Apostles teachings. This was a plan conceived by the devil to steal the truth from the church, and it almost worked. Within 300 years of the founding of the church, there existed the Roman Catholic Church. This church changed many truths into false traditions. The teachings of the Roman Catholic Church are based on the teachings of certain men referred to as 'Church Fathers'.

One of the earliest fathers was Justin Martyr, who in 133 A.D. became a Christian after studying the philosophies of Socrates and Plato. Justin said there was no difference between Christianity and these philosophies; that Christianity fulfills the highest aspirations of Plato (9). Justin also said that the Bible and Plato agreed (10). Justin called Socrates, whose name means 'mighty savior', a "Christian before Christ"(11). This is the same Socrates who said his teachings were from false gods and demons. Although the Catholic Church does not regard all of Justin's teachings, they admit, "His influence is marked above all in Iraenaeus, Tertullian, Hippolytus, and Origen, (other Catholic Church fathers) who built on foundations laid by him"(12). The New Catholic Encyclopedia says, "Justin's Platonism seriously affects his theology of the relationship between the Father and the Logos"(13).

In 185 A.D. Origen, who is mentioned above, declared that, "all truth is precious, whether in Greek or Christian soil... He recognized in the revived Plato a powerful ally of Christianity"(14). Origen "used the philosophy of the Greeks as the vestibule through which to admit his hearers into the temple of the gospel"(15).

Jesus said, "Beware of false prophets, which come to you in sheep's clothing, but inwardly they are ravening wolves" (Matthew 7:15). All philosophers were required to wear a special coat when fulfilling their office. It was a coat made of sheep's wool. These philosophers were the ones Jesus was speaking of. Justin Martyr even wore this coat. Origen said he used the philosophies of these men to show people the gospel. Unfortunately these philosophies originated, not in heaven, but in hell.

Socrates called one of his lords "Apollo". In the book of Revelation 9:11, the angel of the bottomless pit is called by two names. One of them is Abaddon, the Hebrew word for destroyer. The other name is Appolyon, which is the very same as Apollo. The devil is the man who gave Socrates his ideas and philosophies. Many of the Catholic Church Fathers used these philosophies to form Church doctrines, including "The Trinity".

The Regeneration of the Christian And the Holy Spirit

In 325 A.D., the Council of Nicaea established that the Father and Son were separate. The champion of this Council was Athanasius. This man is a highly esteemed church father and his name is derived from Athena, the Greek goddess Plato called the World-Spirit. There was another Council held at Constantinople. At this Council, men determined that the Holy Spirit was also separate from the Father and the Son. Thus the concept of the Trinity was born.

In 354 A.D. a man named Augustine was born. He is one of the most notable of the church fathers. He laid many of the foundations for the Roman Catholic Church. Many regard him as the founder of Christian tradition in the western world. The New Catholic Encyclopedia tells us that Augustine was given certain books written by Plato. While reading them he had a spiritual awakening that changed his vision of the world. These books also led him to a better understanding of God, and led him to the notion of "The Trinity"(16). He later devoted his life fully to Catholicism, but never forsook these philosophies. He believed that "the basis for faith was found in Christ, and the basis for reason was the philosophy of Plato"(17). Please note that his revelation of the Trinity came not from the Bible, but from reading Plato.

By the time Augustine died, most of the truths of the Book-of-Acts Church had been buried under the teachings of these Church Fathers. These church Fathers did not get their understanding from God, or the Bible. They used the philosophies of Greek men who lived hundreds of years before Christ.

Jesus said, "Wide is the gate...which leadeth to destruction"(Matthew 7:13). The name Plato comes from a Greek word 'platus' which means "wide"(18). These Church Fathers were allowing this scripture to be fulfilled through their teachings. They based much of their philosophies and teachings, including "The Trinity", on the teachings of Plato. Plato was instructed by Socrates. Socrates had wisdom given to him by Greek gods, who Socrates referred to as demons. Is this where the Church should get its doctrines?

NO!! The Bible plainly says that: "God was manifested in the flesh" (1 Timothy 3:16); that "God was in Christ reconciling the world unto himself"(1 Corinthians 5:19); that Jesus Christ was "the only begotten God"(John1:18, Amplified and original Greek).

Men have been led astray by the vain philosophies of the world. They have tried to explain God using man's philosophies. James said that the wisdom of the world is, "earthly, sensual, devilish" (James 3:15). The word devilish literally means "proceeding from or resembling a demon"(19). This is the very way Socrates got his wisdom.

Jesus did not say He was the second person in a trinity. He said, "I am the first and the last"(Revelation 1:7). You deserve to know the Truth. "The Trinity" is not based on Truth; it is a doctrine that is a deception of the devil.

"Hear O Israel, the Lord our God is One Lord" Deuteronomy 6:4

WHERE DOES THE TRINITY COME FROM

REFERENCES

(1) Plato, The Republic, Book 4, 496

(2) Plato, Euthydemus, 272

(3) Plato, Apology, 31

(4) Plato, Euthydemus, 302

(5) Plato, Cratylus, 398

(6) New Catholic Encyclopedia, Vol 4, 537

(7) Time-Life Books, Classical Greece, 18

(8) Ibid., Appendix, The Olympian Family

(9) New Catholic Encyclopedia, Vol 8, 94

(10) New Catholic Encyclopedia, Vol 8, 94

(11) New Catholic Encyclopedia, Vol 8, 94

(12) New Catholic Encyclopedia, Vol 8, 95

(13) New Catholic Encyclopedia, Vol 8, 95

(14) John Fletcher Hurst, History of The Christian Church, 300

(15) John Fletcher Hurst, History of The Christian Church, 304

(16) New Catholic Encyclopedia, Vol 1, 1043

(17) New Catholic Encyclopedia, Vol 8, 1063

(18) Vine, Unger, and White, Vine's Expository Dictionary of

Biblical Words, 742

(19) Vine, Unger, and White, Vine's Expository Dictionary of Biblical Words, 158

Now the facts have been laid down before you and I; the argument of discussion that raises many difficult questions continues every day of our lives. How can God be both one and three? Is the Trinity a contradiction? If Jesus is God, why do the Gospels record instances where He prayed to God? While we cannot fully understand everything about the Trinity (or anything else), it is possible to answer questions like these and come to a solid grasp of what it means for God to be three in one. I ask you to pray and see within the spirit how God the creator originated this plan by we serve a mysterious God.

WHY DID THE HOLY SPIRIT COME?

The Holy Spirit came to bear witness to the Lord Jesus Christ and to glorify Him (John 16:13, 14). As Jesus had come to exalt and reveal the Father, the Holy Spirit was sent to exalt and glorify the Son, Jesus Christ.

It Logically follows, then, that the more we allow the Holy Spirit to control our lives, the more we shall love and serve the Lord Jesus Christ, and the more we shall be conscious of His loving and abiding presence.

When we are filled with the Holy Spirit we are filled with Jesus Christ Thus, when we are filled with the Holy Spirit – the Lord Jesus Christ – a power much greater than our own is released within us and through us for service and victorious living.

HOW IS THE HOLY SPIRIT RELATED TO EVERY CHRISTIAN?
JESUS SHOWED HIMSELF ALIVE

See Matt. 28:9, on the resurrection appearances of Christ.

A Christian is one who has received Jesus Christ into his life as Lord and Savior, according to John 1:12; John 3:5; & 2 Corinthians 5:17.

- At the time of spiritual birth:
  - The Holy Spirit regenerates men (John 3:5).
  - The Holy Spirit comes to dwell within each Christian (1 Corinthian 3:16).
  - The Holy Spirit seals every Christian in Christ (Ephesians 1:13; & 4:30).

The Regeneration of the Christian And the Holy Spirit

- ➢ The Holy Spirit is the earnest or guarantee of the inheritance that each Christian will one day receive (2 Corinthians 5:5).
- ➢ The Holy Spirit Baptizes each Christian into the Body of Christ (1 Corinthians 12:13; Galatians 3:27; & Romans 6:3, 4).
- ➢ The Holy Spirit fills every yielded Christian for service.

At the moment of spiritual birth every Christian is regenerated, indwelt, sealed, guaranteed, baptized and filled with the Holy Spirit. The act of regenerating, indwelling, and sealing, guaranteeing and baptizing the Christian into the Body of Christ by the Holy Spirit is a positional relationship and may or may not be accompanied by an emotional experience.

These truths do, however, acquaint the Christian with the thrilling fact of his union with Christ, you in me, and I in you (John 14:20). We exchange our weakness for His power, our sinfulness and defeat for His holiness and victory.

As a result of this relation with Christ, every Christian has the potential to witness with power and to live a life of victory over sin. His potential power, the life of Jesus Christ in every believer, is released by faith as the Christian surrenders the control, his life to the Holy Spirit. Since it is the ministry of the Holy Spirit to glorify Christ, Jesus Christ now has unhindered opportunity to work in and through the believer to perform

His perfect will. Every Christian must be filled with the Holy Spirit in order to have the power to be a more effective witness for Christ. But you shall receive power when the Holy Spirit has come upon you; and you shall be my witnesses both in Jerusalem, and in all Judea and Samaria, and even to the remotest part of the earth. Acts 1: Every Biblical reference to the filling of the Holy Spirit, in both the Old Testament and in the New Testament, is related to power for service and witness.

The response to the filling of the Holy Spirit may vary from a calm assurance of power and quiet realization of a greater faith in Christ and the promises of His Word to a more emotional experience.

A careful study of 1 Corinthians 12 teaches us that all Christians are members of the Body of Christ. As various parts of the human body have different functions, so various members of Christ's body will have different responsibilities in His Kingdom. No Christian should be little another's gift.

Neither should any Christian seek to imitate another in the experience of filling or in the gifts of the Holy Spirit. Every Christian must leave the assignment of the gifts, and the manner in which they are revealed, to the Holy Spirit.

Further, according to 1 Corinthians 13, any or all of these gifts will profit little unless we are motivated by love.

The Regeneration of the Christian And the Holy Spirit

We are admonished by God in Ephesians 5:17-20, (so then do not be foolish, but understand what the will of the Lord is. And do not get drunk with wine, for that is dissipation, but be filled with the Spirit, speaking to one another in psalms and hymns and spiritual songs, singing and making melody with your heart to the Lord; always giving thanks for all things in the name of our Lord Jesus Christ to God, even the Father.

The Apostle Paul was suggesting that a Spirit-filled Christian will know God's will, and may give the impression of being Spirit-intoxicated because of the joy, radiance, boldness and courage that he frequently demonstrates. Also, as this scripture passage suggests, a Spirit-filled Christian is continually praising God in his heart and giving thanks for all things. He realizes, in a way that he could not while in his carnal state, that all that he is and has is by the grace of God.

Beginning with the day of Pentecost and continuing through the centuries, the work of God has always been accomplished through men who were filled with the Holy Spirit — men such as Peter, Paul and all of the disciples.

In more recent times there have been men and women like Apostle Priscilla Burks, Bishop Dr. Jonathan Greer II, Bishop Moses Afful Sr., Bishop Debbie Jordan, Bishop Kenton Stephenson, Bishop Mack Jones, Bishop Michael Hutton-wood, Pastor Bernice Hutton-wood, Apostle Mary Winfrey, Rev. Dwight Foster, Pastor Kenneth Johnson, Pastor Edward

Clothier, Pastor Larry Howard, Pastor Gregory Goode, Pastor Minton, Elder Moses Afful Jr., Apostle Wanda Williams, Mother Gwen Fox, First Lady Deidra Level and scores of other Christian leaders – some of whom are now living – who have been filled with the Holy Spirit and who have been greatly used to further the cause of Christ and His Kingdom. However, the filling of the Holy Spirit is not limited to Christian leaders, but is available to all Christians who meet God's terms.

Here are some sayings about the importance of every Christian's being filled with the Holy Spirit:

Men ought to seek with their whole hearts to be filled with the Spirit of God. Without being filled with the Spirit, it is utterly impossible that an individual Christian or a church can ever live or works as God desires.

Christians are as guilty for not being filled with the Holy Spirit as sinners are for not repenting. They are even more so, for as they have more light, they are so much, the more guilty.

The Spirit – filled life, that life that permits His fullness in a sustained overflow, is the only life that can please God.

The great purpose in the filling of the Holy Spirit is power for service. The best and most used Christians known to me have been men who have testified to a deeper experience of the tilling of the Holy Spirit.

I believe that it is impossible for any Christian to be effective either in his life or in his service unless he is filled with the Holy Spirit who is God's only provision of power.

I wish again to make it especially clear at this point that the Holy Spirit already indwells every believer and the special endowment of power that attends the filling of the Holy Spirit is not reserved for Christian leaders only. Every Christian not only has the prerogative of being filled with the Holy Spirit, but every Christian is admonished to be filled with the Spirit (Ephesians 5:18).

Therefore, if a Christian is not filled, he is disobedient to the command of God and is sinning against God.

Further, since God commands us in His Word to be filled with the Spirit, we may be certain that He has the power to fill us the very moment we invite Him to do so.

Acts 1:4 Gives Us the Promise of the Father

The gift that the Father promised (Joel 2:28-29; Matt. 3:11) is the baptism in the Holy Spirit. The fulfillment of that promise, however, is described as being filled with the Holy Ghost 2:4. Thus, baptized in the Spirit and filled with the Spirit are at times used interchangeably in Acts.

This Baptism in the Holy Spirit should not be identified with receiving the Holy Spirit at regeneration. These are two distant works of the Spirit, often separated by a period of time.

Acts 1:5 Gives With [In] the Holy Ghost

The preposition with is the translation of the Greek word en and is often translated as in Hence, many prefer the rendering ye shall be baptized in the Holy Ghost. Likewise, baptized with water may be translated baptized in water. Jesus Himself is the one who baptizes His believers in the Holy Spirit (see John 1:33).

I assure you that, according to the promises of the Word of God and from observations and personal experience, Jesus is far more eager to give His love and forgiveness, His power for service, and a life of victory over sin than we are to receive them. Jesus is far more eager to fill us with the Holy Spirit than you and I are to be filled.

Why, then, are so many Christians living in defeat? Why are so few Christian's effective witnesses for Christ? Why are so few Christians living lives that are filled with the Holy Spirit? These questions bring us to the next important step in preparation for being filled with the Spirit.

What Is the Spirit – Filled Life?

The Spirit – filled life is the Christ-filled life. The spirit – filled Christian is one who, according to Romans 6:11, has considered himself to be dead to sin, but alive to God in Christ Jesus. Christ is now on the throne of the life. He is Lord! The Holy Spirit came to exalt and glorify Jesus Christ. In order to be filled with the Holy Spirit a Christian must be dead to self. When he is dead to self, the Lord Jesus Christ, who now has unhindered control of his life, can begin to express His love through him. The one to whom all power in Heaven and in earth is given, and in whom dwells all the fullness of the Godhead bodily, can now express that power through the Spirit-filled Christian. The one, who came to seek and to save the lost, now begins to seek the lost through the Christian. He directs the Christian's steps to those who are lost and to those who are in need. He begins to use the Christian's lips to tell of

His love. His great heart of compassion becomes evident in the Spirit-filled life.

Actually, in a very real sense, the Christian gives up his life, his impotence and defeat for the power and victory of Jesus Christ. This is what Pastor Cecil Level referred to as the "exchanged life". When a Christian is filled with the Holy Spirit, he is filled with Jesus Christ. He no longer thinks of Christ as one who helps to do some kind of Christian task but, rather, Jesus Christ does the work through the Christian. He does not want us to work for Him. He wants us to let Him do His work through us. This is that glorious experience that the Apostle Paul knew when he said in Galatians 2:20, "I have been crucified with Christ; and it is no longer I who live, but Christ lives in me." The Christian's body now becomes Christ's body to use as He wills; the mind becomes His mind to think His thoughts; the will is now controlled by His will; the total personality, time and talents are now completely His.

The beloved Apostle goes on to say, and the life which I now live in the flesh I live by faith in the Son of God, who loved me, and delivered Himself up for me. Whose faith? The faith of the son of God: the one who loved us and gave Himself for us. The one to whom "all power in heaven and earth is given. Think of it! Can you grasp what this means? If you can, and if you yield your will to God the Holy Spirit and acknowledge that Jesus Christ is in your life moment by moment, you are in for a great adventure. The Lord Jesus Christ will begin to draw scores of lost men and women to Himself through your yielded, Spirit-filled life.

Why Are So Few Christians Filled With The Holy Spirit?

Basically, the problem involves the will. Man is free moral agent. He was created by God with a mind and will of his own.

God would be breaking His own spiritual laws if He forced man to do His bidding. At the time of conversion the will of man is temporarily yielded to the will of God. In Romans 10:9, Paul tells us that, "if we confess with our mouths Jesus as Lord, and believe in our hearts that God has raised Him from the dead, we shall be saved". Man must be willing to repeat, which means to turn from his own way to go God's way, before he can become a child of God. However, after conversion, the heart frequently loses its "first love". The radiance and glow that accompanied the spiritual birth experience are gone, and many Christians no longer walk in the light as He Himself is in the light (1John 1:7). They no longer seek to do the will of God, but for various reasons, have chosen to go their own way. They have chosen to work out their own plan and purpose for life. Believing themselves to be free, they become servants of sin and finally they say with the Apostle Paul in Romans 7:19, 20, 24 "For the good that I wish, I do not do; but I practice the very evil that I do not wish. But if I am doing the very thing I do not wish, I am no longer the one doing it, but sin which dwells in me. Wretched man that I am! Who will set me free from the body of this death? There is no one more miserable than a Christian out of fellowship with Christ.

In this spiritual condition there is no longer any joy in the Christian walk, no longer any desire to witness for Christ, no concern for those who are desperately in need of the forgiveness and love of our Savior.

What are the reasons, then that one who has experienced the love and forgiveness that only Christ can give, one who has experienced the joy of His presence, would reject the will of God and choose to go his own way? Why would a Christian sacrifice the power and dynamic of the Spirit-filled life in order to have his own way?

There are several reasons:

A. *Lack of knowledge of the Word of God*: God's Word contains glorious truths concerning the relationship that the Christian has with the Lord Jesus Christ God the Father and the Holy Spirit. This lack of information has kept many from appropriating the fullness of the Holy Spirit. Think of it every Christian is a child of God (John 1:12). His sins have been forgiven and he may continue to be cleansed from all sin (1 John 1:7) as he continues in fellowship with Christ. God the Father, Son and Holy Spirit actually dwell in the heart of every Christian, waiting to empower and bring each child of God to his full maturity in Christ

B. *Pride*: Pride has kept many Christians from being filled with the Holy Spirit. Pride was the sin of Satan (Isaiah 14:12-14). Pride was the first sin of man as Adam and Eve wanted to be something they were not. Pride is at the root of most of man's self-imposed estrangement from God. The self centered, egocentric Christian cannot have fellowship with God: for God is opposed to the proud, but gives grace to the humble (1 Peter 5:5).

C. *Fear*: Fear of man keeps many Christians from being filled with the Holy Spirit. "The fear of man brings a snare" (Proverbs 29:25). One of the greatest tragedies of our day is the general practice among Christians of conforming to the conduct and standards of a non-Christian society. Many are afraid to be different ashamed to witness for the one "who loved us and gave Himself for us". Remember, in 1 Peter 2:9 we are told: "But you are a chosen race, a royal priesthood, a holy nation, a people for God's own possession, that you may proclaim the excellencies of Him who has called you out of darkness into His marvelous light "The Lord favors those who fear (reverence which leads to obedience) Him" (Psalm 147:11). Jesus said, "For whoever is ashamed of me and my words, of him shall the Son of Man be ashamed" (Luke 9:26). Many Christian are fearful of being though fanatical by their fellow Christians and others should they be filled with the Holy Spirit.

D. *Secret sin*: Un-confessed sin keeps many Christians from being filled with the Holy Spirit. Perhaps God has reminded you of a lie you have told that has damaged someone's reputation; or stolen merchandise or money that has not been returned; or an unethical transaction; or cheating on an exam or any number of acts that He wants you to confess to Him. He may lead you to make restitution to those whom you have wronged (Matthew 5:23, 24). If so, be obedient to His leading. We may be able to hide these things from our friends and others, but we cannot hide them from God. "Would not God find this out? For, He knows the secrets of the heart (Psalm 44:21). Is there anyone whom you have not forgiven? If so, God will not forgive you (Mark 11:24-26). However, if we confess these sins to God as the Lord directs us, we are forgiven and cleansed (1 John 1:9).

E. Worldly–mindedness: A love for material things and a desire to conform to the ways of a secular society keep many Christians from being filled with the Holy Spirit. "Do not love the world, nor the things in the world. If anyone loves the world, the love of the Father is not in him. For all that is in the world, the lust of the flesh, and the lust of the eyes and the boastful pride of life, are not from the Father, but is from the world. And the world is passing away, and also its lusts; but the one who does the will of God abides forever" (1 John 2:15-17). Man lives a brief span of years and is gone from this earthly scene. Every Christian should make careful and frequent evaluation of how he invests his time, talents and treasure in order to accomplish the most for the cause of Christ. "Only one life will soon be past; only what's done for Christ will last."

"No one can serve two masters; for either he will hate the one and Jove the other, or he will hold to one and despise the other. You cannot serve God and Mammon. But seek first His kingdom, and His righteousness; and all these things shall be added to you" (Matthew 6:24, 33).

F. Lack of trust in God: This keeps many Christians from making a full surrender of their wills to Him and from being filled with the Holy Spirit. Many Christians have a fear that amounts almost to superstition that, if they surrender themselves; fully to God, something tragic will happen to test them. They may fear that they will lose a loved one. Some fear that God will send them to some remote section of the world as a missionary to some savage tribe, against their wills.

I remember well a young lad who had such fears - he was afraid that God would change his plans. As we reasoned together, I reminded him that God's love was so great that He sent His only begotten Son to die for his sins. We spoke of a Savior who loved him so much that He gladly gave His life on the cross and shed His blood for his sins. Then I asked the question, "Can you trust a God like that?" He replied, "I had never thought of it that way - I can and will trust Him." Today this young man has finished seminary. He is one of the most fruitful and victorious Christians I know.

You can trust God with your life, your loved ones, your money, your future, everything! Not only is He a loving Father, but also God s love is wiser than that of any earthly father and is tendered than that of any earthly mother. So do not be afraid to trust God with your whole life, every moment of every day, and He will fill you with His Holy Spirit.

I have two sons and one daughter whom I love dearly. Suppose, when they were very young, they had come to me and said, "Daddy, we love you and have been thinking about how we can show our love for you. We have decided that we will do anything that you want us to do." Now, how would I have responded? Would I have said, "children, I have been waiting for just this moment. Now that you have relinquished your wills to mine, I am going to lock you in your rooms, give away all your favorite possessions, and make you do all of the things that you most dislike to do. You will regret the day you were born. I will make you the most miserable children on this block."

How ridiculous! I would have responded by trying to demonstrate my love for them in an even greater way. In the same way, our heavenly Father is ready to bless and enrich our lives the moment we yield our wills, our all, to Him.

These and many other experiences of defeat have kept Christians from experiencing the joy of the Spirit-filled life.

For example, do any of the following apply to you?

- An exalted feeling of your own importance
- Love of human praise
- Anger and impatience
- Self-will, stubbornness, un-teach-ability
- A compromising spirit
- Jealous disposition
- Lustful, unholy actions
- Dishonesty
- Unbelief
- Selfishness
- Love of money, beautiful clothes, cars, houses and land.

Some of you may wonder, "Is it necessary for me to gain victory over all of my defeats and frustrations before I can be filled with the Holy Spirit?" Absolutely not! Just as Jesus Christ is the only one who can forgive your sins, so the Holy Spirit is the only one who can give victory and power.

How Can A Christian Be Filled With The Holy Spirit?

First, we need to know that just as people have many different experiences when they receive Jesus Christ as Lord and Savior, so they have different experiences when they are filled with the Holy Spirit. For example, one-man responds to the invitation to receive Christ in an evangelistic crusade, another kneels quietly in the privacy of his home and receives Christ. Both are born again, and their lives are changed by the power of Christ. Of course, there are scores of other circumstances and experiences through which sincere men meet the Savior and become "new creatures in Christ."

In like manner, and in different ways, sincere Christians are filled with the Spirit. It should be made clear at this point that to be "filled with the Spirit" does not mean that we receive more of the Holy Spirit, but that we give Him more of ourselves. As we yield our lives to the Holy Spirit and are filled with His presence, He has greater freedom to work in and through our lives, to control us in order to better exalt and glorify Christ.

God is too great to be placed in a man-made mold. However there are certain spiritual laws that are inviolate. Since the Holy Spirit already dwells within every Christian, it is no longer necessary to "wait in Jerusalem" as Jesus instructed the disciples to do, except to make personal preparation for His empowering. The Holy Spirit will fill us with His power the moment we are fully yielded. It is possible for a man to be at a quiet retreat and become filled with the Holy Spirit. It is likewise possible for a man to be filled with the Holy Spirit while walking down a busy street in a great city. Such was the experience of Pastor Cecil Level. It is even possible for a man to be filled with the Holy Spirit and know something wonderful has happened, yet be completely ignorant at the time of what has actually taken place, provided he has a genuine desire to yield his will to the lord Jesus Christ.

I do not want to suggest that the steps, which I am about to propose, are the only way in which one can be filled with the Holy Spirit. This spiritual formula is offered, first, because it is scriptural, and second, because I know from experience that it works.

Do you want to be filled with the Holy Spirit? What are your motives? Are you looking for some ecstatic experience, or do you sincerely desire to serve the lord Jesus Christ with greater power and effectiveness? Do you want, with all of your heart, to help others find Christ?

This is the spiritual formula that I urge you to prayerfully consider:

A. *We are commanded* to be *filled with the Spirit.*

"And do not get drunk with wine, for that is dissipation, but be filled with the Spirit" (Ephesians 5:18). This is an admonition of God. Do you think that He would ask you to do something beyond that which you are able to experience?

B. *We shall receive power for witnessing when we are filled.*

"But you shall receive power when the Holy Spirit has come upon you; and you shall be my witnesses both in Jerusalem, and in all Judea and Samaria, and even to the remotest part of the earth"

Acts 1:8 YE SHALL RECEIVE POWER

This is the key verse in the book of Acts. The primary purpose of the baptism in the Spirit is the receiving of power to witness for Christ, in order to win the lost to Him and to teach them to observe all that Christ commanded. The end result is that Christ may be known, loved, honored, praised, and made Lord of God's chosen people (Mat. 28: 18-20; Luke 24:49; John 5:23;15:26-27).

1. "Power" (Gk. *dunamis)* means more than strength or ability; it designates especially power in action. Luke (in his Gospel and in Acts) emphasizes that the Holy Spirit's power included the authority to drive out evil spirits and the anointing to heal the sick as the two essential signs accompanying the proclamation of the kingdom of God (Acts 6:8; 8:4-8.12-13,10:38; 14:3; 19:8-12; Luke 4;14,18,36; 5:17; 6:19; 9;1-2). The baptism in the Holy Spirit is God's provision for releasing the power of the Holy Spirit into the believer's life.
2. Note that in this verse Luke does not relate the baptism in the Holy Spirit to personal salvation and regeneration, but to the power within the believer to witness with great effect.

3. The Holy Spirit's principal work in witnessing and proclamation concerns the saving work of Christ and His resurrection, and His coming upon believers with power. *See* next note for an examination of how the Spirit witnesses and what that means in our personal lives. 1:8 YE SHALL BE WITNESSES. The baptism in the Holy Spirit not only imparts power to preach Jesus as Lord and Savior (see previous note), but also increases the effectiveness of that witness because of a strengthening and deepening relationship with the Father, Son, and Holy Spirit that comes from being filled with the Spirit (John 14:26; 15:26-27).

4. The Holy Spirit discloses and makes more real to us the personal presence of Jesus (John 14:16-18). Any witness to an intimate fellowship with Jesus Christ Himself will result in an ever growing desire on our part to love, honor, and please our Savior.

5. The Holy Spirit witnesses to "righteousness" (John 16:8, 10) and "truth" (John 16:13) which "glorify" Christ (John 16:14), not only with words, but also in life and deeds. Thus, we who have received the witness of the Holy Spirit to the redemptive work of Jesus Christ will necessarily manifest Christ likeness, love, truth, and righteousness in our lives (1 Cor. 13).

6. The baptism in the Holy Spirit is the initiation point whereby Spirit-filled believers receive the power to witness for Christ and to bring conviction of sin, righteousness, and judgment upon the lost (see John 16:8, note). The effects of such conviction will be evident both in those who sincerely proclaim the message and in those who receive it.
7. The baptism in the Holy Spirit can be given only to those whose hearts are turned toward C in repentance from their wicked ways. It is maintained by the same sincere commitment to Christ (see 5:32).
8. The baptism in the Holy Spirit is a Baptist into the Spirit who is holy ("spirit of holiness, Rom. 1:4). Thus, if the Holy Spirit is truly an in us in all His fullness, we will live in great conformity to Christ's holiness. In light of these Scriptural truths, therefore, we who have been baptized in the Holy Spirit will have an intense desire to please Christ in what every way we can. That is, the fullness of the Spirit complements (completes, fills up) the saving: and sanctifying work of the Holy Spirit in our lives. Those who claim the fullness of the Holy Spirit, yet: live a life contrary to the Spirit of holiness; are misled, deceived, and untruthful. Those who display spiritual gifts, miracles, spectacular signs, or inspiring oratory, yet lack a life of true faith, love, and righteousness, are

operating not by the Holy Spirit, but by an unholy spirit not of God (Mat. 7:21-23; Mat. 24:24; 2 Cor. 11:13-15)

ACTS 1:14 CONTINUED ... IN PRAYER AND SUPPLICATION

The experience of Pentecost always involves human responsibility. Those needing the Spirit's outpouring for power to do God's work should make themselves available to the Holy Spirit through commitment to the will of God and through prayer (Acts 2:4; 2:38; 9:11-17; 40:29-31; Luke 11:5-13;24:49). Notice the parallels between the Spirit coming upon Jesus and the Spirit coming upon the disciples.

(1) The Spirit descended upon them after they had prayed (Luke 3:21-22; Acts 1:14; 2:4).
(2) There were observable manifestations of the Spirit (Luke3:22; Acts 2:2-4).
(3) The ministries of both Jesus and the disciples began after the Spirit came upon them (compare Mat. 3:16 with 4:17; Luke 3:21-23 with 4:14-19; Acts 2:14-47).

If you have no desire to be Jesus Christ's witness or if you have no power in your witness, you may be sure that you are not filled with the Holy Spirit The Holy Spirit came in order for the disciples - and for you and me - to receive power. Why do we need power? To be Christ's witnesses right where we are: and in the remotest part of the earth. Can you sincerely say that this is your motive for wanting to be filled with the Spirit?

C. *If any man is thirsty, let him* come to me *and drink.*

"Now on the last day, the great day of the feast, Jesus stood and cried out, saying, 'If any man is thirsty, let him come to me and drink. He who believes in me, as the Scripture said, "From his innermost being shall flow rivers of living water." But this He spoke of the Spirit, whom those who believed in Him were to receive; for the Spirit was not yet given, because Jesus was not yet glorified" (John 7:37-39). "Blessed are those who hunger and thirst for righteousness, for they shall be satisfied" (Matthew 5:6).

When a Christian is ready to respond to the gracious invitation of our blessed Savior, "If any man is thirsty, let him come to me and drink," he is ready to relinquish his will for the will of God. Therefore, this third step involves a complete surrender of your will, without reservation, to the will of God. You have come to the place where you joyfully anticipate knowing and doing His will because you know God is loving and trustworthy and that His will is best.

Up until this moment the Holy Spirit has been just a "guest" in your life, for He came to live in you the moment you became a Christian. Sometimes He was locked up in a small closet, while you used the rest of the house for your own pleasure.

Now you want Him to be more than a guest - as a matter of fact, you want to turn over the title deed of your life to Him and give Him the keys to every room. You invite the Holy Spirit into the library of your mind, the dining room of your appetites, the parlor of your relationships, the game room of your social life. You invite Him into the small hidden rooms where you have previously engaged in secret, shameful activities. All of this is past. Now, He is the Master! The challenge of Romans 12: 1, 2 has become clear and meaningful to you and you want to "present your body a living and holy sacrifice, acceptable to God, which is your spiritual service of worship." And you no longer want to be conformed to this world, but you want to be transformed by the renewing of your mind, "that you may prove what the will of God is, that which is good and acceptable and perfect"

Now you know that your body is the temple of the Holy Spirit who lives within you. You are not your own anymore for you were bought with the precious blood of the Lord Jesus; therefore, you now want to glorify God in your body and in your spirit, which are God's (1 Corinthians 6:19, 20).

Now, with all of your heart, you want to seek first the kingdom God (Matthew 6:33). Now you want to seek "the things above, where Christ is, seated at the right hand of God. For you have died, and your life is hidden with Christ in God" (Colossians 3:1, 3).

Now you can say with joy unspeakable, as Paul did, "I. have been crucified with Christ; and it is no longer I who live, but Christ lives in me; and the life which I now live in the flesh I live by faith in the Son of God, who loved me, and delivered Himself up for me" (Galatians 2:20).

You have exchanged your life for the life of Christ.

If you can say these things and mean them with all of your heart, you are ready for the fourth step. However, before we take up the discussion of this next step, I feel constrained to call your attention to the words of our Savior found in John 15: 18, 20. "If the world hates you, you know that it has hated me before it hated you. A slave is not greater than his master: If they persecuted me, they will also persecute you."

The Spirit-filled Christian life is not an easy one, though it is a life filled with adventure and thrills, the likes of which one cannot possibly experience in any other way. Whether or not we are Christians, we are going to have problems in this life. Christians or not, we will one day die. If I am going to be a

Christian, I want all that God has for me and I want to be all that He wants me to be. If I am to suffer at all, and one day die, why not suffer and die for the highest and best, for the lord Jesus Christ and His gospel!

Before we leave this thought, let me ask you a question. Have you ever heard of one of God's saints who have suffered for the cause of Christ express any regrets? I never have! I have heard only praise, adoration and thanksgiving to God for the privilege of serving Christ, no matter how difficult the task. On the other hand, I have heard many who have received Christ late in life tell how sorry they are that they waited so long. Do not develop a martyr's complex, but do not expect a "bed of roses" either.

Now, for the next step in receiving the fullness of the Holy Spirit.

D. We *appropriate the filling* of *the Holy Spirit by faith.*

Remember that, if you are a Christian, God the Father, Son and Holy Spirit are already living within you. Great spiritual power and resources are available to you. Like a miser starving to death with a fortune in boxes and jars about his cluttered room, many Christians are starving spiritually, living in defeat, failing to utilize the spiritual fortune that is their heritage in Christ.

In Ephesians 5:18, Paul admonishes, "And do not get drunk with wine, for that is dissipation, but be filled with the Spirit"

Further, in 1 John 5:14, 15, we are assured, "And this is the confidence which we have before Him that, if we ask anything according to His will, He hears us. And if we know that He hears us in whatever we ask, we know that we have the requests that we have asked from Him." We know that it is God's will that we be filled with His Spirit. Therefore, as we ask the Holy Spirit to fill us, we can know according to the Word of God that our prayer is answered.

Like our salvation, the filling of the Holy Spirit is a gift of God - we do not and cannot earn either. Both are received by the complete yielding of our wills, in faith, when we have confessed our sins and met the other conditions.

Here is a review of the steps that we have discussed in preparation for the filling of the Holy Spirit:

1) We are admonished to be filled.
2) We are promised power for service when we are filled.
3) We are to Yield our will to God's will and seek first the kingdom of God.
4) We are to appropriate the filling of the Holy Spirit by faith.

E. We *must expect* to be *filled.*

"And without faith it is impossible to please Him, for he who comes to God must believe that He is, and that He is a rewarder of those who seek Him" (Hebrews 11:6).

Do you believe God wants you to be filled with the Holy Spirit?

Do you believe God has the power to fill you with the Holy Spirit?

In Matthew 9:28, 29, Jesus talked to the blind men and asked of them, "Do you believe that I am able to do this?" They said to Him, "Yes, lord." Then He touched their eyes, saying, "Be it done to you according to your faith."

Find a quiet place where you can be alone and read again the portions of Scripture given in the preceding paragraphs. You do not have to wait for the Holy Spirit. He is already dwelling within you if you are a Christian. He is waiting for you to allow Him to fill you. Remember, "Be is done to you according to your faith." "He is a rewarder of those who seek Him."

Have you honestly yielded your life to Christ, your will to His will?

Do you believe that you are filled with the Holy Spirit at this moment? If so, thank Him that you are filled. Thank Him for His indwelling presence and power. Thank Him by faith for victory over defeat and for effectiveness in witnessing. Praise God and gives thanks continually (Ephesians 5:20; 1 Thessalonians 5: 18).

HOW CAN A CHRISTIAN KNOW WHEN HE IS FILLED WITH THE HOLY SPIRIT?

There are two very good ways of knowing when you are filled with the Holy Spirit.

First: by the promises of the Word of God;
and second: by personal experience.

If you have faithfully yielded to the will of God and sincerely surrendered your way to Him in accordance with the steps outlined in this book, if you have asked Him to fill you he has done it! "And this is the confidence which we have before Him, that, if we ask anything according to His will, He hears us. And if we know that He hears us in whatever we ask, we know that we have the requests that we have asked from Him" (1 john 5:

14, 15). Is it His will that you be filled, according to Ephesians 5:18? Then, can you believe that He has heard you?

Now, can you know that you have the petitions that you desired of Him?

God's Word promises us that we can know. Therefore, on the basis of His Word you can know that you are filled, if you have met the conditions, which are given in His Word.

What about feelings? You may or may not have an emotional response at the time you kneel in prayer and ask or the filling of the Spirit. In counseling with many Young men and women, as well as adults, I have found that the majority experience a calm assurance that they are filled, and with this assurance come a spirit of expectancy that God is going to use them in a way they have never been used before to introduce others to Christ. Greater faith in God and His Word is born in the hearts of those who have been filled with the Holy Spirit. They produce greater results, faith, power, boldness, and effectiveness in witnessing.

First: there is the fact of God's promise in His Word. Then there is the exercise of faith in the trustworthiness of God and His promises. Feeling, Remember, follows faith in the fact: fact, faith and feelings - in that order.

WHAT RESULTS CAN ONE EXPECT FROM BEING FILLED WITH THE HOLY SPIRIT?

Now, here comes the real test that will determine if you are truly filled with the Holy Spirit. As time goes on, do you find that you have a greater love for Christ? Are you more concerned for those who do not know His love and forgiveness? Are you experiencing a greater faith, boldness, liberty and power in witnessing? If so, you are filled with the Spirit. Jesus Christ is beginning to express His life and love through and in you.

I. REGENERATION

(JOHN 3:3) "Jesus answered and said unto him, Verily, verily, I say unto thee, Except a man be born again, he cannot see the kingdom of God.

The Regeneration of the Christian And the Holy Spirit

The Holy Spirit is also called:

Spirit of God ....1 Corinthians 3:16

Spirit of Christ ....Romans 8:9

Spirit of Life ....Romans 8:2

Spirit of Truth.......................John 16:13

Spirit of Grace ....Hebrews 10:29

Spirit of Promise ....Ephesians 1:13

In John 3:1-8, Jesus discusses one of the fundamental doctrines of the Christian faith: regeneration (Tit. 3:5) or spiritual birth. Without the new birth one cannot see the kingdom of God, receive eternal life and salvation through Jesus Christ.

The following are important facts concerning the new birth.

(1) Regeneration is a re-creating and transformation of the person (Roth. 12:2; Eph. 4:23) by God the Holy Spirit (John 3:6; Tit. 3:5). Through this process eternal life from God Himself is imparted to the believer (John 3:16; 2 Pet. 1:4; 1 John 5:11), and he becomes a child of God (John 1:12; Rom. 8:16-17; Gal. 3:26) and a new person (2 Cor. 5:17; Col. 3:9-10). He no longer conforms to this world (Rom.12:2), but is now created after God "in righteousness and true holiness" (Eph. 4:24).

(2) Regeneration is necessary because apart from Christ, all people, by their inherent natures, are sinners, incapable of obeying and pleasing God (Ps. 51:5; Jer. 17:9; Rom. 8:7-8; 1 Cor. 2:14; Eph. 2:3).

(3) Regeneration comes to those who repent of their sin, turn to God (Mat. 3:2), and place personal faith in Jesus Christ as Lord and Savior (see John 1:12).

(4) Regeneration involves a transition from an old life of sin to a new life of obedience to Jesus Christ (2 Cor. 5:17; Gal. 6:15; Eph. 4:23-24; Col. 3:10). The one who is truly born again is set free from the bondage of sin (see John 8:36; Rom. 6: 14-23) and receives a spiritual desire and disposition to obey God and follow the leading of the Spirit (Rom. 8: 3-14). Those born again live righteous lives (1 John 2:29), love other believers (1 John 4:7), avoid a life of sin (1 John 3:9; 5:18), and do not love the world (1 John 2:15-16).

(5) One born of God cannot make sin a habitual practice in his life (see 1 John 3:9). That is, one cannot remain a child of God without a sincere desire and victorious endeavor to please Him and to avoid evil (1 John 1:5-7). This is accomplished only through the grace given

to the believer by Christ (1 John 2:3-11, 15-17,24-29; 3:6-24; 4:7-8,20; 5:1), through a sustained relationship with Christ (see John 15:4, and through a dependence on the Holy Spirit (Rom. 8:2-14).

(6) Those who do live in immorality and follow the world's ways, whatever they profess, demonstrate that they are still un-regenerated and children of Satan (1 John 3:6-10).

(7) Just as one can be born of the Spirit by receiving the life of God, he can also extinguish that life by ungodly choices and unrighteous living, and hence, die spiritually. Scripture affirms, "if ye live after the flesh, ye shall die" (Rom. 8:13). Thus, sin and the refusal to follow the Holy Spirit extinguish the life of God in the soul of the believer and causes spiritual death and exclusion from the kingdom of God (Mat. 12:31-32; 1 Cor. 6:9-10; Gal. 5:19-21; Heb. 6:4-6; 1 John 5:16).

(8) The new birth cannot be equated with physical birth, for the relationship of God with the believer is a matter of spirit rather than flesh (John3:6). Hence, while the physical tie of a father and son can never be annulled, the father and son relationship which God desires with us is voluntary and not indissoluble during our proba-

tionary time on earth (see Rom. 8: 13). Our membership in God's family remains conditional on our faith in Christ throughout our earthly existence, demonstrated by a life of sincere obedience and love (Rom.8:12-14; 2 Tim. 2:12).

II. THE REGENERATION OF THE DISCIPLES

(JOHN 20:22) "And when He had said this, He breathed on them, receive ye the Holy Ghost".

The importation of the Holy Spirit by Jesus to His disciples on resurrection day was not the baptism in the Spirit as experienced by them at Pentecost (Acts 1:5;2:4). It was rather an infusing of the disciples for the first time with the regenerating presence of the Holy Spirit and with new life from the risen Christ.

(1) During the last discourse that Jesus had with His disciples before His trial and crucifixion, He promised them that they would receive the Holy Spirit as the One who would regenerate them: "he dwelleth with you, and shall be in you"(John 14: 17). Jesus now fulfills that promise.

(2) That John 20:22 refers to regeneration can be inferred from the phrase, "he breathed on *them.*" The Greek word for "breathed" *(emphusao)* is the same verb used in the Septuagint (the Greek translation of the O.T.) at Gen. 2:7, where God "breathed into his [Adam's] nostrils the breath of life; and man became a living soul." It

is the same verb that is found in Ezek. 37:9, "Breathe upon these slain, that they may live." John's use of this verb in John 20:22 indicates that Jesus was giving the Spirit in order to bring forth life and a new creation. That is, just as God breathed into physical man the breath of life and he became a new creation (Gen.2:7), so Jesus now breathed into the disciples spiritual life and they became a new creation. Through His resurrection, Jesus became a "quickening [life-giving] spirit" (1 Cor. 15:45).

(3) The words "receive ye the Holy Ghost" establishes that the Spirit, *at that historical moment,* entered and began to dwell in the disciples. The verb form for "receive" is aorist imperative (Gk. *labete,* from the word *lambano),* denoting a single act of reception. The Holy Spirit was given to regenerate them, to make them new creatures in Christ (2 Cor. 5: 17). This "receiving" of life from the Holy Spirit preceded both their receiving the authority of Jesus (John 20:23) and their baptism in the Holy Spirit on the day of Pentecost (Acts 2:4).

(4) Prior to this time, the disciples were technically true believers and followers of Jesus and were saved according to the old covenant provisions. Yet they

were not regenerated in the full new covenant sense. Not until this point did the disciples enter into the new covenant provisions based on Jesus' death and resurrection (see Mat. 26:28; Luke 22:20; 1 Cor. 11:25; Eph. 2:15-16; Heb. 9:15-17). It was also technically at this time and not at Pentecost that the church was born. The spiritual birth of the first disciples and the birth of the church are one and the same.

(5) This passage is crucial in understanding the Holy Spirit's ministry to the people of God. These two statements are true:

   (a) The disciples received the Holy Spirit (were indwelt and regenerated by the Holy Spirit) before the day of Pentecost; and

   (b) The outpouring of the Holy Spirit upon them in Acts 2:4 was an experience occurring after their regeneration by the Holy Spirit. Their baptism in the Spirit at Pentecost was, therefore, a second and distinct work of the Spirit in them.

(6) These two separate and distinct works of the Holy Spirit in the lives of Jesus' disciples are normative for

all Christians. That is, all believers receive the Holy Spirit at the time of their regeneration, and afterwards must experience the baptism in the Holy Spirit for power to be His witnesses (Acts 1:5,8; 2:4; see 2:39).

(7) There is no Scriptural foundation to suggest that Jesus' bestowal of the Holy Spirit in John 20:22 was simply symbolical prophecy of the coming of the Holy Spirit at Pentecost. The use of the aorist imperative for "receive" (see above) denotes reception at that moment and in that place. What occurred was a historical reality in space and time, and John records it as such.

III. BAPTISM IN THE HOLY SPIRIT

(ACTS 1 :5) "For John truly baptized with water; but ye shall be baptized with the Holy Spirit not many days hence".

One of the cardinal doctrines of Scripture is the baptism in the Holy Spirit (see Acts 1:4, note on reading "baptism *in*" rather than "baptism with" the Holy Spirit). Concerning the baptism in the Holy Spirit, the Word of God teaches the following.

- **(1)** The baptism in the Spirit is intended for all who profess faith in Christ, have been born again, and have received the indwelling of the Holy Spirit.

- **(2)** One of Christ's key goals in His mission on earth was to baptize His people in the Holy Spirit (Mat. 3:11; Mark 1:8; Luke 3:16; John 1:33). He instructed His disciples not to begin witnessing until they were baptized in the Holy Spirit and endued with power from on high (Luke 24:49; Acts 1 :4-5,8). Jesus Christ Himself did not enter His ministry until He had been "anointed ... with the Holy Ghost and with power" (Acts 10:38; Luke 4:1; 18).

(3) The baptism in the Holy Spirit is an operation of the Holy Spirit distinct and separate from His work of regeneration. Just as the sanctifying work of the Spirit is a distinct work complementing the regenerating work of the Spirit, so the baptism in the Spirit complements the regenerating and sanctifying work of the Spirit. On the day of Christ's resurrection He breathed on His disciples and said, "Receive ye the Holy Ghost" (John 20:22), indicating that regeneration and new life were being given to them. Then later He told them they must also be "endued with power" by the Holy Spirit (Luke 24:49; Acts 1:5, 8); For the disciples it was clearly a post-regeneration experience (see Acts 11:17). One can be regenerated and indwelt by the Holy Spirit, but still not be baptized in the Holy Spirit (see Acts 19:6).

(4) To be baptized in the Spirit means to be filled with the Spirit; (compare Acts 1:5; 2:4). However, this baptism occurred only at and after Pentecost. Concerning those filled with the Holy Spirit before Pentecost (e.g. Luke 1:15,67), Luke does not use the term baptized in the Holy Spirit. This experience occurred only after Christ's ascension (Luke 24:49-51; John 16:7-14; Acts 1:4).

The Regeneration of the Christian And the Holy Spirit

(5) In the book of Acts, speaking with tongues as the Spirit gives utterance is the initial outward sign accompanying the baptism in the Holy Spirit (Acts 2:4; 10:45-46; 19:6). Baptism in the Holy Spirit is linked so closely with the external manifestation of speaking in tongues that this should be considered the norm when receiving that baptism.

(6) The baptism in the Holy Spirit will bring the personal boldness and power of the Holy Spirit into the believer's life in order to accomplish mighty works in Christ's name and to make the believer's witness and proclamation effective (Acts 1:8; 2:14-41; 4:31; 6:8; Rom. 15:18-19; 1 Cor. 2:4). This power is not some impersonal force, but is a manifestation of the Holy Spirit by which the presence, glory, and works of Jesus ate present with His people (John 14:16-18; 16:14; 1 Cor. 12:7).

(7) Other results of a genuine baptism in the Holy Spirit are:

(a) Prophetic utterances and praise (Acts 2:4, 17; 10:46; 1 Cor. 14:2);

(b) enhanced sensitivity to sin that grieves the Holy Spirit, a greater seeking after righteousness which conforms to Christ, and a deeper awareness of the judgment of God against all ungodliness (see John 16:8, note; Acts 1:8, note);

(c) A life which glorifies Jesus Christ (John 16:13-14; Acts 4:33);

(d) New visions (Acts 2:17);

(e) A manifestation of the various gifts of the Holy Spirit (1 Cor. 12:4-11);

(f) A greater desire to pray and intercede (Acts 2:41-42; 3:1; 4:23-31; 6:4; 10:9; Rom. 8:26);

(g) A deeper love and understanding of the Word of God (John 16:13; Acts 2:42); and

(h) An increasing awareness of God as one's Father (Acts 1:4; Rom. 8:15; Ga1.4:6).

(8) The Word of God cites several conditions, by which the baptism in the Holy Spirit is given,

(a) We must accept by faith Jesus Christ as Lord and Savior and turn from sin and the world (Acts 2:38-40; 8: 12-17). This response involves surrendering our wills to God ("to them that obey him," Acts 5:32). We must turn from that which offends God before we can become "a vessel unto honor, sanctified, and meet for the master's use" (2Tim. 2:21).

(b) We must desire to be filled. Christians should have a deep hunger and thirst for the baptism in the Holy Spirit (John 7:37-39; Is. 44:3; Mat. 5:6; 6:33).

(c) We often receive it in answer to definite prayer (Luke 11:13; Acts 1:14; 2:1-4; 4:31; 8:15, 17).

(d) We should expect that God will baptize us in the Holy Spirit (Mark 11:24; Acts 1 :4-5).

(9) The baptism in the Holy Spirit is sustained in the believer's life by prayer (Acts 4:31), witness (4:31, 33), worship in the Spirit (Eph. 5:18-19), and a sanctified life (see Eph. 5:18). However powerful the initial coming of the Holy Spirit upon the believer may be, if this does not find expression in a life of prayer, witness, and holiness, the experience will soon become a fading glory.

(10) The baptism in the Holy Spirit occurs only once in a believer's life and points to the consecration of the believer unto God's work of witnessing in power and righteousness. The Bible teaches that there may be new filings with the Holy Spirit after the believer has been baptized in the Holy Spirit (see Acts 4:31, note; cf. 2:4; 4:8,31; 13:9; Eph. 5:18). Thus, the baptism in the Spirit brings the believer into a relationship with the Spirit that is to be renewed (Acts 4:31) and maintained (Eph. 5:18).

JOHN 14; 12, GREATER *WORKS;* It is Jesus' purpose and desire that His followers do the works that He did.

(1) The "greater works" include both the work of converting people to Christ and the performing of miracles. This is shown in the narratives of Acts (Acts 2:41, 43; 4:33; 5:12) and in Jesus' declaration in Mark 16:17-18.

(2) The reason for the "greater works" of the disciples is that Jesus will go to His Father, send forth the power of the Holy Spirit (see v. 16; 16:7; Acts1:8; 2:4), and

answer prayer in His name (v. 14). The disciples' works will be "greater" in number and scope.

JOHN 14; 13 ASK IN MY NAME. Prayer in the name of Jesus involves at least two things:

(1) Praying in harmony with His person, character, and will;
(2) Praying with faith in Him and His authority, and with the desire to glorify both the Father and the Son (Acts 3:16). Praying in the name of Jesus, therefore, means that Jesus will honor any prayer that He would have prayed Himself. There is no limit to the power of prayer when addressed to Jesus or the Father in faith according to His desire (see Mat.17:20)

JOHN 14; 16 I WILL PRAY THE FATHER. Jesus will pray that the Father will give the Comforter only to those who are serious about their love for Him, and their devotion to His Word. Jesus uses the present tense in v. 15 ("If ye love me"), thus emphasizing a continuing attitude "of love and obedience.

JOHN 14:16 COMFORTER. Jesus calls the Holy Spirit "another Comforter." "Comforter" translates the Greek *parakletos,* meaning literally "one called alongside to help." This is a rich word, meaning Comforter, Strengthener, Counselor, Helper, Adviser, Advocate, Ally, and Friend. The Greek word for "another" is *allon,* meaning "another of the same kind," rather than *heteros,* meaning another of a different kind. In other words, the Holy Spirit continues what Christ Himself did while on earth.

(1) Jesus promises to send *another* Comforter. The Holy Spirit will do for the disciples what Christ did for them while He was with them. The Spirit will be by their side to help and strengthen them (Mat. 14:30-31), to teach the true course for their lives (v. 26), to comfort in difficult situations (v. 18), to intercede in prayer for them (Rom. 8:26-27; 8:34), to be a friend to further then-best interest (v. 17), and to remain with them forever.

(2) The word *parakletos* is applied to the Lord Jesus in 1 John 2: 1. Therefore Jesus is our helper and intercessor in heaven (Heb. 7:25), while the Holy Spirit is our indwelling helper and intercessor on earth (Rom. 8:9, 26; 1 Cor. 3:16; 6:19; 2 Cor. 6:16; 2 Tim. 1:14).

JOHN 14:17; THE SPIRIT OF TRUTH. The Holy Spirit called "the Spirit of truth" (15:26; 16:13; 3:36; 14:21, 23; 15:8-10,13-14; Luke 6:46-49; 1 John 4:6; 5:6), because He is the Spirit of Jesus who is the truth. As such, He bears witness to the truth

(18:37), enlightens concerning the truth, ex-is untruth (16:8), and guides the believer into (16:13). Those who support the sacrifice for the sake of unity, love, or any other in deny the Spirit of truth whom they claim to dwelling in them. The church which abandons the truth abandons itself. The Holy Spirit will not be the Comforter of those who are indifferent to the faith or halfhearted in their commitment to the truth. He comes *only* to those who worship the Lord "in spirit and in truth" (4:24).

JOHN 14:17 WITH YOU, AND SHALL BE IN YOU. The Holy Spirit now abides with the disciples, and it promises them that in the future He shall in you." This promise of the indwelling of the Spirit was fulfilled after Christ's resurrection. He breathed on them and said to them, "Receive ye the Holy Ghost" (20:22).

JOHN 14:17 I WILL COME TO YOU. Jesus reveals If to the obedient believer through the Holy Spirit, who makes known the personal presence of Jesus in and with the one who loves Him (v. 21). The Spirit makes us aware of the nearness of Jesus, the reality of His love, His blessing, and His help. This is one of His primary tasks. Christ's coming to us by the Spirit should result in a response of love, worship, and devotion.

JOHN 14:21 HE THAT HATH MY COMMAND'S Keeping the commandments of Christ is for those who would have eternal life (John 3:36; 14:21,23; 15:8-10, 13-14; Luke 6:46-49; James :22; 2 Peter 1 :5-11; 1 John 2:3-6).

(1) Obedience to Christ, though never perfect, must nevertheless be real. It is an essential aspect of saving faith, springing from our love for Him (John 14, 21, 23-24; see Mat. 7:21). Without love for Christ, trying to keep His commandments becomes legalism.

(2) To the person who loves Christ and strives to keep His commandments consistently, Christ promises a special love, grace, favor, and His deepest inward presence (John 14:23).

JOHN 14:23 WE WILL ... MAKE OUR ABODE WITH HIM. Those who truly love Jesus and obey His words will experience the immediate presence and love of the Father and the Son. The Father and the Son come to believers by means of the Holy Spirit (see v. 18). It should be noted that the Father's love is conditioned on our loving Jesus and being loyal to His Word.

JOHN 14:24 HE THAT LOVETH ME NOT The person who does not keep the teachings of Christ does not have a personal love for Him, and without love for Jesus true saving faith does not exist (1 John 2:3-4). To say that a person remains saved even though he ceases to love Christ and begins to live a life of immorality, blasphemy, cruelty, murder, drunkenness, sorcery, etc., directly contradicts these and other words of Jesus concerning love, obedience, and the indwelling of the Holy Spirit.

JOHN 14:26 HOLY GHOST The Comforter is identified here as the "Holy Ghost." For the N.T. Christian the most important thing about the Spirit is not His power (Acts 1:8), but that He is "Holy." His holy character, along with the manifestation of that holy character in the lives of believers, is what matters most (Rom. 1:4; Gal. 5:22-26).

Remember, Jesus promised that we would receive power after the Holy Spirit has come upon us. After receiving power we will naturally want to be His witnesses wherever we are (Acts 1:8).

It is definitely true that you will have a greater love for Christ, for your fellowman and for the Word of God when you are filled with the Holy Spirit. Also, the fruit of the Spirit, as described in Galatians 5:22, 23, will become more evident in your life.

However, we must remember that there is a difference between the fruit of the Spirit and the gifts of the Spirit.

The filling of the Holy Spirit is given for power and boldness in witnessing for Christ. Many Christian leaders would somewhat agree, with this statement, "I have tone through my Bible time and time again checking this subject and I make this statement without the slightest fear of successful contradiction that there is not one single passage in the Old Testament or the New Testament where the filling with the Holy Spirit is spoken of, where it is not connected with testimony for service."

We hasten to add that as a Christian abides in Christ, living in the fullness of the Spirit, the fruit of the Spirit - love, joy, peace, patience, kindness, goodness, faithfulness, gentleness and self-control, listed in Galatians 5 :22,23 - is developed and the Christian becomes more mature spiritually. The maturing of the fruit of the Spirit is a lifetime process, which goes on continually as Christ is being formed in the life of the Christian. Some Christians give greater evidence of the fruit of the Spirit than do others, because of a greater degree of yielded-nest to His working. The more we acknowledge ourselves to be dead to sin and give allegiance to the Lord Jesus Christ and His life within us, and the more we allow Him through the power of the Holy Spirit to live out His life through us, the more evident will be the fruit of the Spirit.

The development and maturing of the fruit of the Spirit is a long process, but the gifts of the Holy Spirit are given at the time a person becomes a Christian. Though every Christian who is filled with the Spirit receives power for witnessing, not every

Christian receives the same gift, according to 1 Corinthians 12. Some are called to be apostles, some prophets others evangelists, pastors and teachers (Ephesians 4:11):

Therefore, we must let the Lord direct us into His place of service for us. Do not try to imitate the ministry of someone else. Be patient. Do not try to decide what you should do with your life or where you should serve Christ. He will express His life in and through you as you continue to study His Word and remain obedient and sensitive to the leading of the Holy Spirit. Through God's Word and the leading of the Holy Spirit, you will discover what God's will is for you.

IS THERE MORE THAN ONE FILLING OF THE HOLY SPIRIT?

Yes, there are many fillings of the Spirit for the yielded Christian. We should be filled for each new opportunity of Christian service. The admonition to be filled with the Holy Spirit in Ephesians 5: 18 literally means, in the original Greek, to be filled with the Spirit constantly and continually - to keep on being filled. The Scriptures record several instances where Peter and the disciples where filled with the Spirit.

HOW CAN A CHRISTIAN CONTINUE TO BE FILLED WITH THE HOLY SPIRIT?

The Christian is utterly and wholly dependent upon the Holy Spirit for all spiritual victory and power. Therefore, the more yielded he is, the more liberty the Holy Spirit will have in working through his life in bringing others to Christ and bringing him to spiritual maturity in Christ.

Here are some *practical suggestions that will* assist *you* to *live in the fullness* of *the Spirit:*

A. Meditate on these glorious truths: Jesus Christ literally dwells with in you. You are dead to self and sin and to all personal and selfish desires. You are alive to God through Jesus Christ (Romans 6: 11). Remember, you have exchanged your life with all of sin, frustrations and defeats for the victorious and triumphant life of Christ, in whom all the fullness of deity dwells in bodily form, and in Him you have been made complete (Colossians 2:9, 10). Just think, the one who dwells in your heart is the one who claims all power in heaven and in earth! This is why the apostle Paul said I can do all things through Him who strengthens me. (Philippians 4:13). You have buried "Old Adam," screwed, the lid down on the coffin and covered him over with six feet of sod. Jesus Christ is not helping you to live the Christian life with your old sin nature. Rather He is now using your body as His Temple, your mind to think His thoughts, your heart to express His love and compassion, your lips to speak His truths.

His, will has become your will. At first you may find it necessary to acknowledge and confirm many, many times during the day that this transaction has taken place. You may find it necessary to change your whole way of thinking and praying. Don't think, "What can I do for Christ?" or pray, "God, use me to do this or that for you." Pray rather, "Lord Jesus, I am yours totally and completely without reservation. Use me as you wish. Send me wherever you will, for I am dead and my life is hid with Christ in God." Seek to abide in Christ (I John 2:6). What is involved in abiding in Christ? Jesus said, "If you keep my commandments, you will abide in my love." (John 15:10).

To abide is to keep His commandments. To keep His commandments is to obey. The abiding life is an effortless life. How slowly do we arrive at this simple fact, that true New Testament living is effortless?

A branch does not try to produce fruit, any more than the electric light bulb tries to shine. Neither has any need to try; they simply draw upon an inexhaustible supply of life and energy. In doing so they scarcely touch the fringe of their resources, the Christian has infinitely greater resources. The one who created vegetable life and electric energy is the one who lives in us. Why do we need to try? Only because we are not

The Regeneration of the Christian And the Holy Spirit

---

abiding, the truest test of Christian living is, am I trying or am I abiding? If I find myself still trying, I am not as yet a UN choked channel through which His life may flow.

Meditate on the following portions of Scripture: John 14, 15 and 16; Matthew 6; Colossians 3; Ephesians 5; Romans 6, 8, 12 and 14; 1 Corinthians 13; 1 John 1; Hebrews 11; Galatians 5; and Psalm 37:1-7, 23, 24.

I suggest that you secure a notebook and make an outline of each of these chapters, listing especially those suggestions that you feel will aid you in abiding in Christ. Continue to use your notebook for outlining other portions of Scripture and for recording key verses you would like to memorize. There are many other portions of Scripture that will help you to abide in Christ.

B. Make it a practice to spend definite time each day in prayer for God's guidance of your life and for the souls of men. Make a list of people whom you would like to have find Christ. Pray for them daily (Ephesians 6:18 and 1 Samuel 12:23).

C. Spend time daily reading and studying the Word of God. Make a practice of memorizing key portions of Scripture (see Hebrews 4:12; 1 Corinthians 2:9-12; Psalm 119: 4, 9, 15, 16, 97, 98, 103, 105, 130).

D. Do not grieve the Holy Spirit. Confess and turn from sinful practices. 1 John 1:9 say; "If we confess our sins, He is faithful and righteous to forgive us our sins and to cleanse us from all unrighteousness." The moment you do something you know is wrong, you will grieve the Holy Spirit if you do not confess it. What do we mean by grieving the Holy Spirit? The Spirit is holy and He is displeased and saddened when a Christian commits sin and continues its practice. Therefore, if you want to continue to be filled with the Holy Spirit and to have power in witnessing for Christ, live a yielded, holy life.

E. Do not quench the Holy Spirit. Be sensitive to the leading of the Holy Spirit for He is omniscient. He has infinite wisdom and knowledge and will lead us into all truth (John 16: 13). Never say "no" to Him. As you grow accustomed to the Spirit-filled, Christ-directed life, you will have many wonderful experiences such as Philip had (Acts 8:26-29) when the Holy Spirit led him to speak to the Ethiopian; and as Paul had (Acts 16:9) when he was called to Macedonia to preach the gospel.

The Voice of the Spirit

The most thrilling experiences of my entire life has always been those times when that still small voice of the Spirit speaks to my heart telling me to speak to God's people about Christ.

In speaking to them; in obedience to the Spirit's leading, I have always discovered that the Holy Spirit had prepared their heart for my witness.

Many times I have been told Cecil the Lord sent you to me or everything you have said has been for me, someone must have told you of my problem.

But over the years I have learned that the Spirit knows all things, and if you and I are filled with His presence and power, we will always have the right words to say to those who are in hurting need.

There have been many such thrilling leadings of the Spirit, but I shall share only one.

One day I was driving to a Church Tent Revival that my Spiritual Father Pastor was having. This revival was been so greatly used of God in the lives of thousands that where attending. It was an extremely hot day late in August and my car developed a vapor lock and refused to run as I started around the expressway. I waited for the motor to cool and finally, after a considerable delay, I got the car started.

I drove into the yard of a nearby home to ask for water to fill the radiator. The man of the house was very generous and gracious. He helped me fill the radiator with water, but even though I was there five or ten minutes, I did not speak to him about Christ. My mind was on the Church Tent Revival that I wanted badly to attend. As I leaned over to pick up the radiator cap, which had blown off, my New Testament fell out of my shirt pocket. Still I did not hear that still, small voice of the Spirit. I had thanked the man for his kindness and was driving out of his yard when suddenly I felt a strong compulsion to return to talk with this man about Christ. "But," I argued as I discussed it, "I am late for the Tent Revival now. Anyway, he would think I was a crackpot if I was to go back. Besides, if I were going to witness to him about Christ, I should have done it when he was helping me fill the radiator with water."

The Regeneration of the Christian And the Holy Spirit

Human arguments are futile against the insistent voice of the Spirit, and after I had driven a couple of miles, I turned around and headed back. As an added precaution I pulled over to the side of the road for prayer. "Lord, don't let me make a mistake - this seems so foolish. Give me the words to say. May your will be done."

As I drove into the yard, the man came out on the porch to greet me. "Did you forget something?" he asked. "Yes, I did forget something, sir. I know this may sound a little strange, but I am a Christian and I felt that the Lord wanted me to come back to talk to you about Christ." There was no need to say more for, as I spoke, tears began to gather and trickle down his cheeks. His chin began to tremble as he told me that he knew the Lord had sent me. He asked me to come inside and as I went in, he called his wife.

He said, "I used to go to church years ago, but I fell into sin and I haven't been back in many years. This week my wife has been attending a tent revival service and more and more, with each passing day, I have been burdened with the weight of my sins. I want to get right with God." We all knelt there in his living room and both he and his wife committed their lives and their home to Christ. I went on my way, praising God for the leading of His Holy Spirit and for another opportunity to witness for our blessed Savior.

The Regeneration of the Christian And the Holy Spirit

As you ask God to fill you with the Holy Spirit, you are about to begin the greatest adventure of your life. Remember that you are asking to be filled with the Holy Spirit rather than filled with self. As He takes control of your life, you will become more like Christ. The Holy Spirit is not the author of confusion and emotional extremes. He has come to exalt and glorify Jesus; therefore, when you are filled with the Holy Spirit, it will be your constant desire to do the will of God and that which will please and honor Jesus Christ.

Why did Jesus come into this world?
To, seek and to save that which was lost" (Luke 19:10).
What will please Him most?

We shall please Him most as we help fulfill His Great Commission, by going into the entire world and preaching the gospel to every creature and letting Him live His life through us.

How is this to be accomplished? By the power of the Holy Spirit Think of it - you and I are privileged to be used by our Savior in helping to reach a lost world with the glorious good news.

We dare not sin against the Lord and against those who are waiting to hear by hesitating another moment Ask Him to fill you now!

CPSIA information can be obtained
at www.ICGtesting.com
Printed in the USA
BVHW051335140922
647021BV00001B/284

9 781613 798126